THE WINGED SERPENT

THE WINGED SERPENT

AMERICAN INDIAN PROSE AND POETRY

Edited by Margot Astrov
With a Foreword by Paul Zolbrod

Beacon Press
Boston

Beacon Press
25 Beacon Street
Boston, Massachusetts 02108-2892

Beacon Press books
are published under the auspices of
the Unitarian Universalist Association of Congregations.

Published by arrangement with
HarperCollins Publisher, Inc.

99 98 97 96 95 94 93 92   8 7 6 5 4 3 2 1

Library of Congress Cataloging-in-Publication Data

The Winged serpent : American Indian prose and poetry / edited by
    Margot Astrov ; with a foreword by Paul Zolbrod.
        p. cm.
    Includes bibiographical references and index.
    ISBN 0-8070-8105-1
    1. Folk literature, Indian—North America—Translations into
English. 2. Folk literature, Indian—Translations into English.
    I. Astrov, Margot, 1908–
E98.F58W56 1992
398.2′0497—dc20   92-13743
                    CIP

CONTENTS

v

CONTENTS

vii

viii

CONTENTS

SECTION TEN: *From Peru*

FOREWORD

I discovered *The Winged Serpent* in the early 1960s while first looking for written transcriptions of oral poetry. In the emerging cultural climate I had begun to question the vaunted manuscript tradition of Western Europe as the sole wellspring of literature and to wonder if print was indeed the only poetic medium. Jack Kerouac and the "Beats" were being read at the time, in anticipation of the cultural revolution of the later sixties and early seventies; the civil rights movement had given new momentum to oratory and song; Alan Lomax was elevating folk music to a higher level of respectability, buttressed by performers like Pete Seeger and Josh White; Albert B. Lord's *The Singer of Tales* demonstrated that classics like *The Iliad* and *The Odyssey* had roots in an enduring oral tradition.

Intrigued by such developments, I spotted Margot Astrov's anthology in a remote Santa Fe bookstore. I was undertaking a search for Navajo and Pueblo storytellers who could help show that poetry was not just something written down in verse and confined to the classroom as an example of high culture, but rather a widely applied art form ultimately fixed in the sound of the human voice. Astrov's volume stood out because it exhibited a clear intimacy with Native American cultures that similar collections lacked.

Once I began my own field research I could admire the way she combined broad-minded enthusiasm with patient fieldwork, extensive scholarship, and close reading to demonstrate that a viable poetic tradition existed in preliterate tribal North America. I found myself benefiting in many ways from the knowledge and insight evident here but missing in other books. I also met other readers who were gradually learning to recognize a Native American literary heritage and who valued this work, which seemed to be circulating quietly as something of an underground classic.

Margot Astrov's anthology of Native American poetic material was first published in 1946 by the John Day Company as *The Winged Serpent*, remaining on their list until 1955 when it went out of print. In 1962, Capricorn Books reissued it with the title *American Indian Prose and Poetry*, perhaps to distinguish it from D. H. Lawrence's *The Plumed Serpent*. It went through several printings and again won quiet respect before disappearing once more. This is a work whose significance calls for renewed attention, however. Given the increased understanding of Native American poetry making in particular and what we now fail to realize about poetry in general, perhaps the time has come at last to establish it as an achievement worthy of endurance.

The Winged Serpent is an outstanding survey of hitherto unnoticed poetic traditions tantamount to those of classical Europe. Yet when first published it seems to have aroused indifference or outright hostility outside its narrow circle of committed readers. The deeper, foreign patterns of Native American thought in the anthology went widely unnoticed, either because critics maintained an overly simplistic view of Native Americans as victimized noble savages or because readers accustomed only to print overlooked the intricacies of orally transmitted songs and narratives.

The few reviews I have located either attacked Astrov's work or oversimplified it. The earliest was a short critique by Mabel Dodge Luhan in *Book Week*, November 10, 1946. There she complains that "the lisping fragments of these translated lines . . . have very little Indian in them." In her hackneyed cry of outrage, though, Luhan fails to acknowledge any of Astrov's vast ethnopoetic knowledge. Underlying her self-righteous objection is the simplistic assumption that a good translation should project a glossy, preconceived vision, as if just one existed for all the tribes. Now that we know more about Native American societies and their poetry making, though, we can appreciate Astrov's early attempt to gather Native American oral material from a recognizably wide array of distinct cultures as a pioneering work of great breadth and profound sensitivity.

As for Margot Astrov herself, born in 1908, she immigrated to New Mexico from Germany in 1940 to escape Hitler's Europe with a husband who soon died, leaving the marriage childless. With her she brought a lifelong interest in Native Americans; she may even have begun compiling this book before coming to the United States. By transferring credits from the University of Berlin, she was able to earn a degree in anthropology from the University of New Mexico in 1944. She then matriculated as a graduate student there but never took an advanced degree, ostensibly because she was out on the reservation both teaching and gathering material, but just as likely because she was skilled at doing research without formal training.

Besides this book, she published only two items that I know of: "The Word Is Sacred," a general essay on Native American poetry in the September 1946 issue of *Asia and the Americas*, and "The Concept of Motion as the Psychological Leitmotif of Navaho Life and Literature," a scholarly study appearing in the *Journal of American Folklore* (1949), which shows how the poetry of a given language is fed by its own innate grammatical structure. With the encouragement of Mary Cabot Wheelwright, the Boston philanthropist and student of Navajo religion, she also recorded a version of the Navajo *Mountain Chant* ceremony during the fall and winter of 1946. The manuscript resulting from that work exists in the archives of the Wheelwright Museum in Santa Fe. An attempt to find a publisher never materialized, which is unfortunate, for that outstanding example of text retrieval illustrates an easy familiarity with sources and field techniques missing from other anthologies of traditional Native American literature.

Beyond that, Margot Astrov prepared nothing else for publication and spent the rest of her active life teaching elementary school first in a small community near Window Rock, Arizona, then in an off-reservation Navajo school at Canoncito, New Mexico, and finally at Tesuque Pueblo north of Santa Fe. She maintained a close circle of friends in this important intellectual and artistic New Mexico community—some of whom earned recognition in their own right as experts on Native American art and culture. Those still living speak warmly of her intellect and scholarship and report that she loved children and was greatly fulfilled in teaching them. Without regard for commercial success or critical acclaim, Astrov took satisfaction in the publication of this book. Modest, retiring, and deeply private in seeking professional fulfillment, she was content to go on teaching and doing research for their own sake. "In her own quiet way, she had a vibrant personality," one of her friends told me with unabashed fondness. "In conversation she could lift you to where you yourself felt as intelligent as she was." Beyond such recognition from close associates, Astrov labored in near obscurity until she suffered a stroke in 1959 and was permanently hospitalized a few years later with an ailment that now sounds like Alzheimer's disease. The last close acquaintance known to have visited her tells of seeing her virtually comatose, unable to recognize anyone or to speak. She finished her life alone and destitute at a public hospital in Las Vegas, New Mexico, where according to officials she died in 1980. Behind her she left only her written work and the fond, devoted memories of a handful of people who enjoy talking about her as much for her personal qualities as for her professional achievements.

2.

Like its editor, then, *The Winged Serpent* deserves ongoing recognition. Although broadly eclectic anthologies can indeed attempt too much with too little understanding, when compiled with Astrov's editorial skill, cultural awareness, and poetic sensibility they offer a great deal. North America's tribal poetry has always been too varied and profound to allow Astrov's efforts to become eclipsed by newly translated, narrowly focused collections from specific tribes.

At first glance, her collection undertakes the same purpose as other broad-based anthologies of introducing a wide range of material, and it repeats weaknesses that inevitably result. Like them, for example, it submits scores of languages and cultures to misleading generalizations. Arranging material by region is a case in point. Astrov groups the Athabascan Navajos and their closely related Apache neighbors with the Hohokam Papagos and Pimas in section three on the one hand and restricts section four to the various Pueblo tribes on the other. Papago and Pima material might just as readily be matched with those of the more northerly Puebloans, however, since those groups all belong to the broad Uto-Aztecan family of languages and share an interconnected prehistoric past. Meanwhile, the Apaches and the Navajos—relative newcomers from the north who entered the region shortly before the Spanish invaded the Rio Grande valley—exchanged poetic traditions with the Pueblos in more recent times. Such distinctions reflect intertribal complexities only now being understood, which says nothing of what they can add to a full understanding of each tribe's distinct history.

Another example of weakness common to these anthologies is the inclusion of earlier English translations by ethnographers sometimes more eager to translate literally or to assemble raw data than to replicate poetry. Those renditions could suppress curiosity over how a single prayer extracted from a healing ceremony or a speech translated into English might have originally sounded in Navajo or Nez Percé, or what the impact of such items might have been when performed in their original tribal setting. By being arrayed page after page where they were never intended to be placed, selections easily take on a silent facelessness, so to speak, fully inimical to what poetry really is—that art form whose primary medium is the sound of the human voice recited in speech and song with or without the help of print.

To be sure, among the pioneer researchers who first began gathering material there were some skilled translators, such as the redoubtable Washington Matthews, or Frances LaFlesche and Herbert Spinden, whose written renditions can sometimes project a transcendent poetic authenticity. But that authenticity might very well emerge from a work's inner quality— which often plays out of the deep structure of the language which produced it—rather than from the way an English translation feels at the surface. As do many of her selections, Astrov's two introductory chapters suggest an alertness to such quality. There and in her footnotes she registers the distinctiveness of various speech communities whose verbal and cultural differences generated poetic features quite unlike those common to conventionally written literature, whether or not they always sounded good in English.

That awareness alone distinguishes this anthology. Ever since Columbus, blind generalizing about the so-called Indians has prevailed: they had no history, no institutions, no cultures equal to those of Europe.

With no books, they had poetic traditions least of all. Together with her footnotes, Astrov's opening commentary safeguards against gross oversights and easy generalizations of that sort. The overall effect is an aggregate of wisdom, good sense, and literary awareness that makes for a milestone of lasting literary discovery. In today's media-driven culture, barriers have arisen between the academic sector and the non-academic, which in turn fosters a culture of specialization with its designated experts and authorities. Poetry has all but disappeared in that climate except as special training exchanged in the classroom. There it is mostly consigned to the silence of print, while what is spoken or sung exists elsewhere as popular culture in an increasingly departmentalized, video-centered electronic age. Gradually—almost insidiously—poetry has ceased to circulate as widely as it once did and its role has become obscured. Originally a ubiquitous art existing at all levels of taste as a means of cultural affirmation in the widest sense, it is now often regarded primarily as an arcane form of intensely individualized reflection requiring special training to be understood or appreciated and having no utilitarian function.

Among tribes such as the Teton Sioux or the Tlingit, poetry has always functioned in a deeply traditional way—not as a finely textured outer fabric or rarefied experience or personal expression, but as something that an entire culture shares; not as a small body of curricular material set aside for experts and acolytes, but as the total means by which a widely shared tradition reinvests itself from one generation to the next in the stories it tells, the songs it sings, the chants and prayers it seeks to perpetuate, and the information and understanding its people must refine and transmit. Poetry has sustained that tradition by preserving and relaying established values and has invigorated it by merging new thinking with old or by drawing borrowed ideas into the culture's inner workings.

Margot Astrov understood all that—more widely perhaps than the fieldworkers Ruth Underhill or Frank Cushing may have when they mastered a single language or participated in the life of a single culture. As linguists do she knew that humankind is the language-using species. As an anthropologist she appreciated the collective dynamics that designated and perpetuated a given culture. And as a critic she also understood that whether in its naturally colloquial idiom or in some more artificially sung or chanted form, language could artistically bond individuals to a group while distinguishing one cultural identity from another.

Look closely at Astrov's introduction to spot how trenchantly she could project that awareness. "It must be kept in mind that language not only influences behavior, but also reflects customary responses and attitudes," she says (p. 6). Such an assertion identifies language's deep human function and helps to explain why human communities need poetry to forge collective awareness, and how it is that each culture employs language in its unique way. To illustrate, Astrov describes how the Kwakiutl use one of two metaphors for marriage. They call it either making "war on the princess" or trying "to get a slave"—thereby revealing their distinctively competitive aggressiveness and their characteristic way of relating in terms of wealth and possession (p. 7). Likewise she mentions how the Zunis personify the earth as a female and call rain "her living waters" in an environment where ongoing life is so dependent upon rainfall (p. 9).

Specifying relationships between marriage and warfare or ownership, or between the sky-borne inseminating rain and the life-giving earthly female, invokes poetry making at its deepest. How such things are expressed grows out of perceptions that somehow gain recognition and that once recognized are verbalized in a communal effort to grasp knowledge and convey awareness. Furthermore, the discovery of relatively simple likenesses leads to the disclosure of more elaborate ones. This book is full of such illustrations in works such as the Kwakiutl prayer, which sees a dead killer whale in terms of a three-way conflict between a fisherman, his rivals, and "Short-Life-Maker Women" (p. 283), or the Tewa weaving song, which portrays the sky as the semen-bearing father, the earth as the receptive mother, and the landscape as a rich tapestry of living offspring (p. 221).

The selections in *The Winged Serpent* show that Native American poetry does not rely on the sound of language alone but on its union with profound significance. The "Speech to the Dead" (p. 151) projects the Fox conception of eschatology as a state wherein departed souls eventually enhance the living by favoring them from the spirit world. The next selection, "Lamentation" (p. 152), then illustrates how intensely the Fox mourn death. And in her accompanying footnote Astrov observes the sharp contrast between the fervor of Fox grief and their stoic acceptance that once gone the dead can be persuaded to bless the living, which is a subtle recognition that memories of those who are gone enrich the lives of those who remain. Translation notwithstanding, when read carefully with Astrov's note these two selections demonstrate how speech and revelation merge. Together discovery and expression make for poesis—the application of an art form that depends upon the medium of language whether written or not.

Able to penetrate linguistic surface, Margot Astrov learned something about how Native Americans used poesis that is overlooked if they are seen only as victims or if their works are judged only for quality of translation. A teacher herself, she nonetheless thought of poetry as more than classroom material; and as someone who lived and worked among Native Americans, she could see in their stories and lyrics more than a social cause. Poetry, she realized, goes deeper. When used poetically language is radical in the literal sense that it designates the most deeply rooted human conceptions without which the loveliest or most forceful expression remains hollow.

All of which is to say that the editor of this fine book knew the difference between deep poetry, literally the radical essence of what those who employ it have traditionally understood and managed to say, and mere surface poetry, what language displays without regard for inner substance. When awkwardly phrased, translation can disfigure the former without destroying it. At the same time, poetry deftly translated but transplanted insensitively from culture to culture can wither at the very root, especially when moved from the loam of oral tradition into print. Margot Astrov may have had to rely on some flawed translations in assembling *The Winged Serpent* but her sensitivity to what the works originally achieved was not compromised.

Native American tribes may differ in their collective visions, just as their verbal depictions of relationships often contrast sharply with European ways of seeing them. Yet whatever the aesthetic cost of wresting the contents of this volume away from their context of actual performance, the pieces combine to display a wide range of valuable perceptions along with deep conceptual concerns. That happens thanks to Astrov's open-minded interest and her breadth of scholarship, to her capacity for observation, and to her deeply ingrained cultural sensitivity. Too much is now known and too much new material now exists to permit the future production of any better single-volume anthology of Native American poetry. Yet recognition of this work is necessary in a pluralistic society like ours struggling to acknowledge its own diversity. Better than any such collection I know, this book celebrates the long-delayed discovery that Native Americans have always been highly poetic.

An Acknowledgment

I acknowledge the following people for their assistance in gathering information about Margot Astrov and *The Winged Serpent*. Thanks first of all to John and Carolyn Adair, who graciously shared their personal recollections with me, as did Priscilla and Robert Bunker, Betty Rosenthal, and Katherine Spencer

Halpern. I also thank Donna Slawsky, librarian at HarperCollins, for helping me trace the publishing history of this book under both its titles; Barbara Rosen, reference librarian at the University of New Mexico, who provided invaluable assistance in my search for primary and secondary published material; and Steve Rodgers, curator at the Wheelwright Museum of the American Indian in Santa Fe, for helping me locate valuable archival material.

Suggestions for Further Reading

Now sometimes identified as *ethnopoetics*, the study of Native American poetry and literature no longer yields a bibliographical guide easily. For up-to-date scholarly material among academic journals, consult *Studies in American Indian Literatures*, along with *American Indian Quarterly, American Indian Research Journal, Sun Tracks*, and the excellent *Sun Tracks* series.

Astrov's bibliography remains a superb list of then-existing translations and commentary on Native American storytelling, verse, and song. While much has subsequently been translated, her bibliography remains the most thorough, citing some of the very first intertribal collections as well as excellent translated material from individual tribes.

Most noteworthy among other early anthologies of Native American poetic material are Natalie Curtis, *The Indians' Book* (New York: Harper and Brothers, 1907, reprinted by Dover, 1968); George W. Cronyn, *The Path on the Rainbow* (New York: Boni and Liveright, 1918, republished by Liveright, 1934, and then by Ballentine, 1962, as *American Indian Poetry: An Anthology of Authentic Songs and Chants*); and A. Grove Day, *The Sky Clears: Poetry of the American Indians* (New York: Macmillan, 1951, reissued by University of Nebraska Press, 1964).

More recent anthologies—all published around the time Astrov reappeared in the John Day catalog—include Jerome Rothenberg, *Shaking the Pumpkin: Traditional Poetry of the Indian North Americas* (Garden City: Doubleday, 1972, reissued in 1991 by University of New Mexico Press); Frederick W. Turner III, *The Portable North American Indian Reader* (New York: Viking, 1974); Gloria Levitas, Frank R. Vivelo, and Jacqueline Vivelo, *American Indian Poetry: We Wait in the Darkness* (New York: G. P. Putnam's Sons, 1973); Thomas E. Sanders and Walter W. Peek, *Literature of the American Indian* (Beverly Hills: Glencoe Press, 1973); Alan Velie, *American Indian Literature: An Anthology* (Norman: University of Oklahoma Press, 1979).

A number of scholarly articles exist that evaluate and/or summarize efforts to translate, compile, and anthologize Native American poetry. Any one of them can help the beginner undertake a detailed study. Some I recommend include Dell Hymes, "Some North Pacific Coast Poems: A Problem in Anthropological Philology," *American Anthropologist*, vol. 67 (1965): 316-41; Dennis Tedlock, "On the Translation of Style in Oral Narrative," *Journal of American Folklore*, vol. 84 (1971): 114-33; Karl Kroeber, "Deconstructionist Criticism and American Indian Literature," *Boundary* 2, vol. 7, no. 3. (1979): 73-89; LaVonne Brown Ruoff, "American Indian Oral Literatures,"

American Quarterly, vol. 30 (1981): 328-38; and Andrew Wiget, "The Study of Native American Literature: An Introduction," in his *Critical Essays on Native American Literature* (Boston: G. K. Hall, 1985). Other book-length collections of essays on Native American literature and poetry include Abraham Chapman, *Literature of the American Indians: Views and Interpretations* (New York: Meridan, 1975); Karl Kroeber, ed., *Traditional American Indian Literatures* (Lincoln: University of Nebraska Press, 1981); Brian Swann, ed., *Smoothing the Ground: Essays on Native American Oral Literature* (Berkeley: University of California Press, 1983); and Brian Swann and Arnold Krupat, eds., *Recovering the Word: Essays on Native American Literature* (Berkeley: University of California Press, 1987).

PAUL ZOLBROD
Allegheny College

ACKNOWLEDGMENTS

It lies in the nature of an anthology that it never can be wholly complete externally. But internally it can be integral for the simple reason that it usually has its source in a personal experience of great intensity: it is this very personal experience that may shape a compilation of many, more or less disconnected, items into the whole of what one could call a personal credo.

At the incipient stage of this collection I benefited greatly from the understanding guidance of the late Dr. Vladimir Astrov, versed in the lore and literature of many peoples.

I am under obligations to Dr. Leslie Spier, professor of anthropology of the University of New Mexico, who, at considerable expense of time, read the manuscript at various stages of completion and aided me with invaluable counsel.

My thanks are due to Professor Clark Wissler of the American Museum of Natural History, to Dr. Herbert J. Spinden of The Brooklyn Museum, and to Professor Ruth Benedict of Columbia University for their kindness in reading the manuscript and for their stimulating comments.

I am especially grateful for the many helpful suggestions by Dr. Clyde Kluckhohn of Harvard and for the encouraging interest shown by Mr. Van Wyck Brooks.

I also wish to express my gratitude toward Mr. Witter Bynner, who kindly read the entire manuscript. I am furthermore indebted to Dr. Robert Lowie of Berkeley University, to Professor Wolfgang Koehler of Swarthmore College, to Dr. Ruth Underhill and Mr. Maurice Ries, Laboratory of Anthropology, for stimulating criticisms and suggestions of various kinds.

Assistance in the preparation of the manuscript has been rendered in various ways by Mrs. Helen Chase, Mrs. Mary von Kramer, Mrs. Margaretta Dietrich, Miss Hester Jones, Mr. Willard Houghland, Miss Dorothy Stewart, Miss C. F. Bieber, and Mrs. Eric J. Reed. My grateful thanks are due to each of them.

Last, but most certainly not least, I wish to express my gratitude toward the various authors, publishers, and executors who most generously granted me the permission for reprint.

In New Mexico, 1946   MARGOT ASTROV

THE WINGED SERPENT

INTRODUCTION

When Old Torlino, a Navajo priest of *hozónihatál*, was about to relate the story of creation to Washington Matthews, he made the following pronouncement, addressing as it were his own conscience, solemnly affirming that he was going to tell the truth as he understood it. And he said:

> I am ashamed before the earth;
> I am ashamed before the heavens;
> I am ashamed before the dawn;
> I am ashamed before the evening twilight;
> I am ashamed before the blue sky;
> I am ashamed before the sun.
> *I am ashamed before that standing within me*
> *which speaks with me.*
> Some of these things are always looking at me.
> I am never out of sight.
> Therefore I must tell the truth.
> *I hold my word tight to my breast.*

This declaration is nothing but a succinct statement of the Indian's relation to the "word" as the directing agency that stands powerfully behind every "doing," as the reality above all tangible reality. It is the thought and the word that stand face to face with the conscience of the native, not the deed.

This anthology of American Indian prose and poetry is a collection made up of translations. With the aborigine's attitude toward the sacredness of the word in our mind, it seems fitting to consider, if only briefly, the problems that the translator confronts in transferring native texts from languages, utterly differing, we are told, from all Indo-European idioms both in structure and function, into our own language. If the native feels deeply responsible in using the word as a tool designed not only to perpetuate but also to actuate, to bring about change, and to create, the translator, in trying to tackle his difficult task, must also be pervaded by a similar sense of responsibility and a compelling obligation toward truthfulness. He, too, must hold the word close to his breast.

In going through a collection like this we will be struck not only by the marked differences in style, but also by the tremendous differences in mental attitudes expressed in these verbal documents.

It is one of the purposes of the present compilation to bring home to the reader that the idea of "the" Indian is an abstraction, though a methodologically helpful one at times. There are Puebleños and desert dwellers; Indians of the plains and the woodlands; tribes that obtain their livelihood on the lonely plateaus or in the mountainous areas west of the prairies. Each of these various tribes has acquired during long stretches of time its own peculiar way of expressing itself, a diversity due mainly to the formative influences of three factors: individual disposition, group configuration, and natural environment.

But we have to take into account still another factor that intensifies the individualizing aspect of the translations. This is the personality of the translator. One might be inclined to consider the fact that he is likely to color somehow the oral expression of the native in a way that may seriously impair the authentic value of the document. This may or may not be the case. It quite depends on the quality—shall we say poetic quality—of the translator. For translation is, if not creative, then re-creative work. It is surely a high art.

Wholly literal translations would do little justice to the original—a mere cursory survey of interlinear renderings would make this plain even to the layman. A creative element has to enter into the process of transmuting an oral expression from the terms of one language into the terms of another. In some way or other the translator has to translate not only the actual words of a myth, a tale, or a song, but also the cultural matrix of which the verbal document to be translated is an organic part. If this is a prerequisite of all translations, how then can it be reconciled with the other requirement: linguistic fidelity to the original sources? That both of these requirements can be met has been demonstrated by a considerable number of outstanding linguists and workers in the field—by Washington Matthews, Cushing, Brinton, Frances Densmore, Sapir, Spinden, Ruth Bunzel, and Ruth Underhill, to name only a few.

There is still another problem of which the reader of translations of primitive poetry should be aware. From translations we can draw little if any conclusions as to the style of a language, its structure, and its peculiar function. It may be for this very reason that a thorough study has not yet been attempted of either aboriginal verse or aboriginal prose. Says Herbert J. Spinden:

Style is so intimately involved in the organic possibilities of a particular language that it cannot, properly speaking, be translated except in so far as it concerns the sequence and arrangements of materials. It can be matched in general effect, and that is about all. In translating poetry, then, the thought and the emotional environment of the thought, can be restated but not the poetic style *per se*.[1]

Ruth Underhill confirms the above statement when she says

A translator of a language so different from ours in all its devices as is an Indian tongue has much to answer for. The entire way of thought is different. So are the grammatical forms and the order of words. One can hope to make the translation exact only in spirit, not in letter . . ." [2]

But even so the translator will be capable of rendering the spirit of a text exactly only when he is thoroughly familiar with the culture to which the document belongs. Ruth Benedict has shown in her analyses of Zuñi mythology how decidedly both the content and structure of a myth, song, or prayer are determined by the culture of which it is a part.[3]

But not only this. The very language that carries tale and song is influenced and formed by the attitudes, beliefs, and customs of a people. It must be kept in mind that language not only influences behavior, but also reflects customary responses and attitudes. To give a few examples: The Kwakiutl have two metaphorical expressions for "marriage." One is "to make war on the princess" and the other, "to try to get a slave." These metaphors, though revealing in themselves, would remain misty to one not acquainted with the cultural make-up of the Kwakiutl. The most out-

[1] *Songs of the Tewa*, 1933, p. 55.
[2] *Singing for Power*, 1938, p. 16.
[3] See also Stanley S. Newman on "Linguistic Aspects of Yokuts Style" in A. H. Gayton and W. Newman: *Yokuts and Western Mono Myths*, Anthropological Records, Un. of Cal., Vol. 5, No. 1, p. 4-6. Berkeley: 1940.

6

standing features of their social behavior are competi-
tive aggressiveness and an inclination to consider all
relations to human and nonhuman environment in
terms of wealth and exclusive ownership. Their whole
vocabulary seems to be flavored by this peculiar sys-
tem of evaluation.[4]

Another example. In an interesting paper B. L.
Whorf sets forth the results of an investigation he un-
dertook concerning the relation of habitual thought
and behavior to language on the part of the Hopi.[5]

A characteristic of Hopi behavior, says Whorf, is the
emphasis on preparation. One has only to read care-
fully the autobiography of Don Talayesva as edited
by Leo W. Simmons in order to find this statement
amply verified. When Don finally came to the conclu-
sion that the white man's ways of education were only
leading him astray, making him helpless in the face of
the difficulties he had to overcome in order to make
a living in his own native environment, all his life
turned into a carefully planned pattern of prepara-
tion. His description of this period of his life is carried
to a vast extent by words designating pursuits of prep-
aration and concentration for the task ahead. One
casual remark on Don's part is very revealing as to this
attitude which is characteristic of most of the Pueblo
people and, in fact, of many other culture groups of
native North America. His statement, "I studied clouds
and paid close attention to my dreams in order to
escape being trapped by storms too far from shelter,"

[4] Franz Boas, *Race, Language and Culture,* New York: The
Macmillan Company, 1940, p. 232.
[5] In Leslie Spier, ed., *Language, Culture, and Personality, Es-
says in Memory of Edward Sapir,* Menasha, 1941, p. 75.

not only discloses plainly this emphasis on preparation, but also reveals another characteristic trait of Hopi culture: the overlapping of two systems of experience which would seem to us to belong to two different planes. To the Hopi the phenomena of what we would call the objective side of the world are intimately interlocked with those of the subjective side of it. And not only do these two forms of experience—with the Pueblo people—sustain each other, but the "inner" world is apt to dominate over the "outer" world. And it is this peculiar outlook that has greatly influenced the language of the Hopi, especially the emphasis he places, as Whorf calls it, on the "intensity-factor of thought." Here again, as among so many tribes, thought is believed to determine and to direct reality. By concentrating his thoughts on the corn plant, for instance, he feels he can influence its growth and maturation. His treasury of verbal expressions is therefore rich in words connoting invisible, intangible, fluctuating factors. Even events and phenomena of the objective world are described in terms of germinating processes, of growth, of unfolding or of vanishing, or as mere outlines, as fleeting colors or as hardly perceptible movements.

Even the layman, therefore, can easily grasp the difficulties with which a translator has to wrestle in trying to transmute a verbal document of such a people into a language the very structure of which, as well as its function, is determined to a considerable extent by an attitude quite different from that of the native people. Take, for instance, the Zuñi. Living in a semi-arid region, their minds dwell upon rain with greatest intensity, and their hearts are made happy by the sight

8

of wandering clouds, the sound of clapping thunder, the flash of lightning zigzagging across the parched fields. Their prayers for life are prayers for rain. And as it is a law pertaining to all magical practices that the more satisfying the description of the desired object, the more satisfying the outcome, one would naturally expect in the vocabulary of a desert-dwelling people delicate nuances concerning climatological factors and atmospheric changes. Thus all of the Pueblo people discriminate between various forms of rain: fine and heavy, female and male, misty and torrential.

Zuñi, we are informed by Ruth Bunzel, is, like Latin, a highly inflected language and therefore very sensitive to skillful handling. It is a poetic language *per se*. While, according to Dr. Bunzel, many characteristic traits of Zuñi poetical style get lost in the process of translation, its vigor and responsiveness to most subtle shades have certainly been preserved in her outstanding translations from the Zuñi language. One prayer may follow as an example—a magic formula rather, recited for the purpose of bringing rain, the greatest good in the desert:

When our earth mother is replete with living waters,
When spring comes,
The source of our flesh,
All the different kinds of corn,
We shall lay to rest in the ground.
With their earth mother's living waters,
They will be made into new beings.
Coming out standing into the daylight
Of their sun father,
Calling for rain,
To all sides they will stretch out their hands.
Then from wherever the rain makers stay quietly

They will send forth their misty breath;
Their massed clouds filled with water will come out
    and sit with us,
Far from their homes,
With outstretched hands of water they will embrace
    the corn,
Stepping down to caress them with their fresh waters,
With their fine rain caressing the earth,
And yonder, wherever the roads of the rain makers
    come forth,
Torrents will rush forth,
Silt will rush forth,
Mountains will be washed out,
Logs will be washed down,
Yonder all the mossy mountains will drip with water.
The clay-lined hollows of our earth mother
Will overflow with water,
Desiring that it should be thus,
I send forth my prayer.[6]

Indian poets of many tribes have been aware of the hypnotic quality of carefully selected words, and they have used it quite consciously. The sleep-inducing formulae Robert H. Lowie recorded in connection with tales he gathered among the Crow and Hidatsa are interesting and worth being quoted here. The formulae —preluded or followed by suggestive statements indicating the fatigue of a person—consist of vivid descriptions of sensual impressions of a visual, auditory, and even kinesthetic order: the rustling of leaves, the monotonous patter of rain striking against the tepee, the booming of high winds, the rippling of a brook, the soothing coolness of shade. These sleep-evoking descriptions, made up usually by the storyteller on the

[6] Ruth Bunzel, *Introduction to Zuñi Ceremonialism*, 47th Annual Report of the Bureau of American Ethnology, p. 484.

spur of the moment, have retained the quality of light opiates even in the translations rendered by Lowie:

At night when we are about to lie down, listening to the wind rustling through the bleached trees, we do not know how we get to sleep, but we fall asleep.

When the day is cloudy, the thunder makes a low rumble and the rain patters against the lodge, then it's fine and nice to sleep, isn't it?

And from a Hidatsa version:

You hear the wind blowing, blowing, then all of a sudden it dies down just as if it had gone off to sleep.

Little playful lullabies they are, these sleep-inducing spells, designed after a pattern a psychotherapist of our days would heartily recommend.

I have said that from translations one cannot perceive the particular style of a language. This statement, however, ought to be modified, since the ever-recurring patterns of stylistic expression may be recognized even from translations. Herbert J. Spinden summarized the essential characteristics of Indian poetry in the following way: [7]

The device of rhyme seems not to have been used by the most cultivated Americans of pre-Columbian times . . . Nor were there any certain stanza forms except such as were brought about by the repetition of phrases. The outstanding feature of American Indian verse construction comes from parallel phrasing, or, let us say, repetition with an increment, which gives an effect not of rhyming sounds but of rhyming thoughts. Sometimes the ceremonial pattern demands a repetition for each world direction with formal

[7] *Songs of the Tewa*, 1933, p. 58.

changes involving the color, plant, animal, and so forth, associated with each station on the circuit.

Rhythm is the repetition of units that are either similar or contrasting. It is said that the pleasure derived from rhythm has, in all probability, a physiological basis and that it corresponds to certain physiological processes, as for instance the contraction and expansion of the respiratory organs, the pulsating of the blood, the beating of the heart. But this drive that forces man to express himself in rhythmic patterns has its ultimate source in psychic needs, for example the need of spiritual ingestion and proper organization of all the multiform perceptions and impressions rushing for ever upon the individual from without and within, especially during his formative years. Among the Indians, this necessity of organization has found conspicuous expression not only in the arts of poetry and prose in the form of various types of repetition, but likewise in the decorative arts of pottery, basketry, and textile designs. Furthermore, repetition, verbal and otherwise, means accumulation of power. In fact, the magically coercive quality that seems to determine the character of most of the prayers, incantations, and songs of the American Indian, is so conspicuous that the other driving force which leads to the iteration of statements—the need of organization—is frequently overlooked. A child repeats a statement over and over for two reasons. First, in order to make himself familiar with something that appears to him to be threateningly unknown and thus to organize it into his system of familiar phenomena; and, second, to get something he wants badly. As the various devices of repetition—

preludes, refrains, burdens, iteration of phrases in part or in whole—are readily translatable in every language, we are well familiar with it.

The principle of organization seems to dominate the poetical construction of most of the ceremonial songs of the Apache; the magically creative quality seems to determine more conspicuously the forms of repetition employed by the Navajos. An example of the latter follows: a corn song supposedly sung by the Home God, who was the first to plant corn. And it is again Washington Matthews who provides us with the translation, preserving the native quality of the song and yet at the same time making it part of our own poetical treasury: [8]

> The corn grows up.
> The waters of the dark clouds drop, drop.
> The rain descends.
> The waters from the corn leaves drop, drop.
> The rain descends.
> The waters from the plants drop, drop.
> The corn grows up.
> The waters of the dark mists drop, drop.

The coercive character of this song seems irresistible indeed, and it is cleverly enhanced by the skillful use of sounds characteristic of rain.

This gift of employing deftly the various sounds produced by surrounding nature—by animal, water, wind, storm-torn woods—is characteristic of Indian poets of many tribes. We find it among the people inhabiting the southwestern deserts, among the dwellers of the Pueblos, and among the tribes of the Northwest.

[8] "Songs of Sequence," in *Journal of American Folk Lore,* VII, 191.

Francis LaFlésche, a Plains Indian, trained anthropologist and understanding recorder of customs and traditions not only of his own tribe, the Omaha, but also of the related Osage, has placed us under obligation by his outstanding translations of native records. All of them seem to be alive and to be carried by the sounds and echoes of nature, by the swirling winds of the plains, by the whisper arising out of shadowed groves in the hour before dawn and the twitter of sleepy birds in the twilight of evening.

An appealing symmetry and rhythm, however, is achieved by the native poet not only onomatopoetically, but also through the use of contrast; for instance, night and day, silence and sound, male and female, immobility and swift movement. In one of the ceremonial Rattle Songs of the Osage, the Black Hawk and the Red Hawk are placed in two opposed verses, forming a balanced pattern in which the native delights. The Black Hawk represents the night and is spoken of first, for, says LaFlésche, "out of the darkness of the night proceed the mysteries of life." The Red Hawk typifies the glowing color of the dawning day, and the various stanzas of this song vivify in interlocking patterns of repetition and parallel phrasing the endless recurrent movement of the coming and going of day and night.

The methods of balance, parallel phrasing, and incremental repetition are also employed in many of the prose compositions of the American Indian. In the recital of mythical stories repetitions are utilized for magical and organizatory purposes. In the art of oratory they are employed, apparently, mainly for the sake of emphasis. How subtly this device may be used even for spontaneously delivered speeches shows in the following fragment of an oration by a warrior about to enter the Warpath with the express desire of dying on his mission. This speech, recorded by R. H. Lowie among the Crow, may also stand as an example of the high art of translating. Crazy-Dog-Wishing-To-Die concludes his speech in this way:

You Above, if there be one who knows what is going on, repay me today for the distress I have suffered. The One Who causes things, Whoever he may be, I have now had my fill of life. Grant me death. My sorrows are overabundant. Though children are timid, they die harsh deaths, it is said. Though women are timid, you make them die harsh deaths. I do not wish to live long; were I to live long, my sorrows would be overabundant; I do not want it.

In reviewing the literary creations of the American Indian from the standpoint of the recorder and translator, we ought to draw the reader's attention to another group of poetical compositions in which the usual devices of repetition, parallel phrasing, metaphorical expression, and imaginative comparison are not employed at all. These songs are, rather, conspicuous for their extreme conciseness both in thought and word. Few of these short songs are complete in themselves and may be regarded as mnemonic summaries of trains of thought familiar both to the singer and to the listeners, or as the highlights of myths and rituals. The Papago informant of Ruth Underhill succinctly summarized the main characteristic of these mere wisps of songs by saying: "The song is so short because we know so much." The singer sketches only a thought or an impression and it is left to the poetical imagination of the listener and his resources of mythic knowledge to supply the gradations of color and mythical context. As an example two Papago songs recorded by Dr. Underhill follow, both superb in their poetical abstraction and both masterpieces of translation.

The Eagle sings:

1. The sun's rays
   Lie along my wings
   And stretch beyond their tips.

2. A gray little whirlwind
   Is trying to catch me.
   Across my path
   It keeps whirling.

These are exquisite and friendly vignettes, indeed, remindful of the best of Japanese Haiku that turn the listener into a poet himself, for it is his part to fill the sketch into completeness. These songs, says Underhill, will make the Papago visualize the eagle with all his peculiarities. Thus his power is asserted, and, being what he is, the superior of man, he will cleanse man from impurities, free him from disease, and ward off death. This is what a song may bring about.

How fortunate the method may be of having aboriginal texts not only recorded but also translated by gifted and trained natives themselves—a procedure recomended repeatedly and most emphatically by Franz Boas—is demonstrated by a number of aboriginal anthropologists, for instance by the already mentioned Francis LaFlésche, by Archie Phinney (Nez Percé), and Ella Deloria (Dakota), to name just a few. The translations of Rasmussen are marked by an unmistakable quality of authenticity because he lived the life of the Eskimo and their language was his language, while

Thalbitzer used the idiom of the Amassalik Eskimo as his second tongue. The method suggested and employed by Frances Densmore, to let carefully selected interpreters do the translation, seems also to be a most fortunate one, as the vast collections of American Indian poetry of F. Densmore herself well prove.

In any case, in reading aboriginal prose and poetry, as it is compiled in this anthology, the reader is at the mercy of the translator, not only for bad but also for good. If the following pages, besides presenting the American Indian as an outstanding poet, as a singer of exquisite songs, maker of sublime prayers or dangerous spells, and judicious teller of tales and mythic stories, present also the recorder and translator as congenial collaborators, this collection has fulfilled its purpose.

Chapter I: *The Power of the Word*

THE MAGIC CREATIVENESS
OF THE WORD

The singing of songs and the telling of tales, with the American Indian, is but seldom a means of mere spontaneous self-expression. More often than not, the singer aims with the chanted word to exert a strong influence and to bring about a change, either in himself or in nature or in his fellow beings. By narrating the story of origin, he endeavors to influence the universe and to strengthen the failing power of the supernatural beings. He relates the myth of creation, ceremonially, in order to save the world from death and destruction and to keep alive the primeval spirit of the sacred beginning. Above all, it seems that the word, both in song and in tale, was meant to maintain and to prolong the individual life in some way or other— that is, to cure, to heal, to ward off evil, and to frustrate death. Healing songs, and songs intended to support the powers of germination and of growth in all their manifestations, fairly outnumber all other songs of the American Indian.

The word, indeed, is power. It is life, substance, reality. The word lived before earth, sun, or moon came into existence. Whenever the Indian ponders over the mystery of origin, he shows a tendency to ascribe to the word a creative power all its own. The word is conceived of as an independent entity, superior

19

even to the gods. Only when the word came up mysteriously in the darkness of the night were the gods of the Maya enabled to bring forth the earth and life thereon. And the genesis of the Uitoto opens, characteristically enough, in this way: "In the beginning, the word gave origin to the Father." The word is thought to precede the creator, for the primitive mind cannot imagine a creation out of nothingness. In the beginning was the thought, the dream, the word.

The concept of the word as Creative Potency lives on, even in the simplest song of hunting or of harvest, of battle, love, or death, as sung by the contemporary Indian.

It is this conscious certainty of the directing and influencing power of the word that gives a peculiar urging force to the following war song as heard by Robert H. Lowie among the Crow Indians: [1]

> Whenever there is any trouble,
> I shall not die but get through.
> Though arrows are many, I shall arrive.
> My heart is manly.

By chanting these words the singer raises himself to a higher level of achieving power; it is the magic quality of these words that will render him invulnerable.

It is not the herb administered to the sick which is considered the essential part of the cure, rather the words recited over that herb before its use. When a Hupa Indian is sick, the priest recites over him the account of a former cure whose central incident is the travel of some mythical person to the ends of the

---

[1] R. H. Lowie, *Crow Religion, Anthropological Papers of the American Museum of Natural History*, XXV (1922), 410.

world to find release from his ailment. It is sufficient, says Goddard in his fine book on the Hupa, that the priest tell how one went: the spirit of the suffering person will follow the words even if he does not comprehend them.

A considerable number of songs of the Indian can be understood only from this firm belief in the word's power to bring about the desired result upon which the singer has fixed his mind.[2]

The word not only engenders courage and power of endurance, but it also is the ultimate source of material success. "I have always been a poor man. I do not know a single song," thus the Navajo informant of W. W. Hill began his account of agricultural practices.

> It is impossible [continues Dr. Hill] to state too strongly the belief as illustrated by that statement. It summed up in a few words the whole attitude of the Navaho toward life and the possibility of success. With respect to agriculture, it was not the vicissitudes of environment that made for successful crops or failures, but the control of the natural forces through ritual.[3]

And, quite logically, the Eskimo hunters think it a mistake to believe that women are weaker than men. For were it not for the incantations sung by the women left behind, the hunter would return without game. Said one hunter to Bogoras: "In vain man walks

[2] Of course, it should be kept in mind that the tune which carries the word is of equal importance and may emanate as much magical power. Poetry, with the American Indian, is not an independent art but exists only in connection with music—that is, as song.

[3] W. W. Hill, *The Agricultural and Hunting Methods of the Navaho Indians*, Yale University Press, 1938, p. 52.

around, searching; but those that sit by the lamp are
really strong, for they know how to call the game to
the shore. . . ."

SONGS OF HEALING

The poetic imagination of primitive man circled,
naturally, with greatest persistency around the mys-
tery of life and death. Physical sickness was experienced
as partial death. When a medicine man committed
himself to a cure, he was conscious of fighting a battle
against death, already present in the suffering indi-
vidual.

His strongest weapon in this fight was the word.

Thus, the chief aim of the *Midé*—the native religion
of the Chippewa—was to secure health and long life
to its adherents, and elaborate initiations and song
series were held during spring, and each member was
expected to attend at least one of these gatherings for
the renewal of his spiritual power.

Each initiate *(Midéwiníni)* had his own set of songs,
some of which he had composed himself and others
which he had purchased for considerable sums of
money or for equal values of goods.

The initiates, we are told, have to go through eight
degrees, which means through a succession of sym-
bolic deaths and resurrections. The following song is
a song a neophyte receives while he is passing through
such a painful experience of ceremonial dying: [4]

[4] Frances Densmore, *Chippewa Music*, I, Bureau of American
Ethnology, Bulletin 45, p. 73.

You will recover; you will walk again.
It is I who say it; my power is great.
Through our white shell
I will enable you to walk again.

And as the initiate revived, the words of this song
will forever retain its healing power: it is the healing
song *par excellence*. Songs with similar words of gen-
tle coercion and firm confidence were chanted all over
the continent—accompanied by the compulsive beat
of the drum. The word heals and restores!

That the curing song may be considered to exert a
twofold function we learn from Leslie Spier. The
Maricopa shaman who is about to practice a cure sings
his songs, which he has received in dreams, in the first
place in order to gain strength himself. The cure itself
is secondary and additional. It further seems as though
healing power was believed a quality inherent in all
song, the inseparable essence of melody and word.

In describing dreams to me [says Dr. Spier] the song was
always mentioned first, as though that was the most signifi-
cant element. The curative powers which the dreamer ac-
quired . . . were sometimes mentioned as adjunct to song.

Which only proves again that song, at least with the
American Indian, hardly exists as a pure art form: it
always serves an end.[5]

The Navajo—shepherds of the Arizona deserts—are

[5] Among the Fox we find the same attitude toward song as a
life-preserving means. Said Owl: "Well, now I shall tell you
about this which we sing. As we sing the manitou hears us. The
manitou will not fail to hear us. It is just as if we were singing
within the manitou's dwellings. . . . We are not singing sportive
songs. It is as if we are weeping, asking for life. . . ." Michelson,
The Owl Sacred Pack of the Fox Indians, p. 57.

beset to a large degree by the fear of the all-pervading powers of evil and death. In this the Navajo, together with the neighboring Apaches, distinguish themselves from most of the other tribes of the American Southwest. Yet these Bedouins of North America are remarkable psychiatrists. All of their ceremonies are prophylactic or therapeutic means to free themselves from the nightmare of dread and inward panic. They are harassed by innumerable fears. Nevertheless, they are placid and gay and gracefully poised people; for they have instituted a cure for every threatening or real disturbance of their mental equilibrium—a cure against the poisonous breath of evil thought; a cure against bad dreams; a cure against every kind of physical ailment; and numerous cures against the impurity of death.

But the evils that are feared most of all are the intangible powers that lurk in the soul of man himself. It is the unknown error and the undiagnosed dread that are really dangerous. But even for this grave internal ailment the Navajo inaugurated a healing ceremony, the evil-chasing chant. This ritual, with its sand paintings, chants, and magic paraphernalia is supposed to absorb the concealed and hidden evil. And, as evil is due to ignorance, a person can be cured by being told the origin of evil, which is the purpose of the Ceremony of the Enemy Way as recorded by Father Berard Haile. And not only will the patient be cured by way of knowledge, he also will have gained power; for, through ritual and song, evil has turned into good—a psychiatric method of transmutation reminiscent of alchemistic processes, indeed.

Above all, however, it is the spirit of creation that

heals. With the aid of his song, the Navajo medicine man submerges the sick or frightened person in the beauty and perfection of primeval creation. With compelling repetitions he sings of the earth and the stars and the growing corn, as they were in the days of origin. Thus the suffering person is placed within the purity of the beginning of all things, when man knew neither sin nor fear and the horror of death. It is of psychological significance that in the Creation Myth, as recorded by Mary C. Wheelwright, fear of death or dying is not mentioned. Rather, the patient (*hatrali*— that is, the man who is "sung over") is made to accept the idea of death, for according to the myth Sun and Moon could not go on living unless every day and every night a person should die.[6]

Or, by way of the magic word, the medicine man is relating the sick person to the companion of the never-ailing gods, who are traveling across the Rainbow from the Mountain of Everlastingness to the Mountain of Unending Happiness. He is made to breathe in the purifying air of sacred places where only gods are wont to abide. And out of the agony of fear and pain he awakes renewed, suffused with divinity and strengthened by the dream-experienced reality of life eternal.

The long song sequences of the curing ceremonies of the Navajo are sacred, and bear the patina of antiquity and the mark of the inward experiences of generations: no word may be altered nor omitted, no gesture of dance and ceremony may be changed.

However, it should be added that the Navajo discriminate between songs that must be sung precisely,

[6] See also Washington Matthews, *Navajo Legends*, Houghton Mifflin, 1897, pp. 80, 223.

with no alterations whatsoever, and the sequence of whole ceremonies. No singer, says Clyde Kluckhohn in his indispensable *Introduction to Navajo Chant Practice,* ever gives two performances of the same chant without some variations: "absolutely precise repetition of any ceremonial behavior is dangerous to the performer." An excellent observation from a psychotherapeutic point of view.

INDIVIDUAL SONGS

Still, there exists another group of songs that may well be noted here, songs born out of the moment of lonely suffering, songs composed by individuals in the subconscious endeavor to soothe the anguished heart by transporting the inward pain into the reality of words.

> It is only crying about myself
> That comes to me in song.

Thus sings an unknown poet high up on the mist-enshrouded coast of the Pacific.

Frances Densmore tells of an old and blind woman who lived among the Nootka of the Northwest Coast. This woman was very poor and homeless and drifted from family to family. She used to sit against the wall of some house all day, singing softly a song like this:

> Sing your song
> Looking up at the sky.

And the people were always glad to have her near and to give her a meal, for she spread happiness wherever she went.

The same author collected among the Chippewa a wee little song, once composed by a child left alone in the wigwam during a long, long night. Now, the great fear of Chippewa children is the owl. And to drive away the gnawing dread of the owl's hooting, the child channeled his terror into the words of a song that he repeated over and over again. This is the literal translation:

> Very much also
> I of the owl am afraid,
> Sitting alone in the wigwam.

The people in near-by tents heard him singing all through the night, and they learned the song and it became quite popular in the village.

Among the Mandan a number of songs have been recorded which did not serve any magical purpose, but were merely the expression of individual longing and loneliness. Thus the work of the scout was often wearisome, and during the long hours of vigil, far away from camp, homesickness sometimes threatened to overcome him. Then the few words of a song, composed there and then, might endow the scenes of camp life with a sense of greater reality and so create the illusion of the longed-for social contact. Sings a scout:

> A certain maiden
> To the garden goes,
> Lonely
> She walks.

At the same time a Mandan woman, whose task it is to watch over the maturing crops, might also be overwhelmed with loneliness and sorrow and sing a song like this:

The man who was my lover
He is dead.
I am lonely.
If I could go to him
I would go—
No matter how far away.

Though no magical healing power is believed to be
inherent in this type of song, these words will have
exerted a healing effect nonetheless, for the "word" as
such heals and restores.

ESKIMO SONGS

Sometimes the song is not thought of as the starting
point of the cure itself, but as a means to induce utter
concentration, indispensable for the sincere medicine
man in order that he may find out the source of some
mental disturbance or physical sickness of some patient.

Knud Rasmussen tells of such an experience he had
among the Iglulik Eskimo. He was enjoying the hos-
pitality of Padloq, the *angakoq,* and his friendly wife
Taqonak. He had arrived at a time when the aging
couple were greatly troubled about the failing health
of the child they had adopted. Rasmussen relates:

One evening Padloq . . . had been particularly occupied
in studying the fate of the child. We were lying on the
bench, enjoying our evening rest, but Padloq stood upright,
with closed eyes, over by the window of the hut. He stood
like that for hours, chanting a magic song with many in-
comprehensible words. But the constant repetition, and the
timid earnestness of his utterance made the song as it were
an expression of the frailty of human life and man's help-
lessness in the face of its mystery. Then, suddenly, after

hours of this searching in the depths of the spirit, he seemed to have found what he sought; for he clapped his hands together and blew upon them, washing them as it were, in fresh human breath, and cried out: "Here it is! Here it is."

We gave the customary response: "Thanks, thanks. You have it."

Padloq now came over to us and explained that Qahitsap had been out in the previous summer in a boat, the sail of which had belonged to a man now dead. A breeze from the land of the dead had touched the child, and now came the sickness. . . .

While the Navajo lead their suffering fellow men back to the days of creation in order to cure them, the Eskimo deem it best to sing healing songs that convey joy. For the helping spirits, they say, avoid contact with human beings who dwell too long on sorrow, and evil prevails where laughter is unknown.

Thus Rasmussen tells further of a women shaman who once received, quite unexpectedly, a song from her helping spirit. These are the words of the song:

> The great sea
> Has sent me adrift,
> It moves me as the weed in a great river,
> Earth and the great weather move me,
> Have carried me away,
> And move my inward parts with joy.

These two verses, says Rasmussen, she was repeating incessantly during a gathering in the large snowhouse —"intoxicated with joy"; and all in the house felt the same intoxication of delight. And without being asked they began to state "all their misdeeds, as well as those of others, and those who felt themselves accused and admitted their offenses obtained release from these by lifting their arms and making movements as if to fling

29

away all evil, all that was false and wicked was thrown away. . . ."

The entrancing repetitions of a song of joy led voluntarily to a catharsis and purification of the soul.

Indeed, fixed anger and stable resentment that find no egress whatsoever are capable of eating up a man's soul, step by step, very slowly and painfully.

The same Iglulik Eskimo devised a most congenial method of giving poisonous grudges a vent—the contest or juridical drum song.

In these duels of abuse the singer endeavors to present his enemy in a ridiculous light, making him the laughing stock of the assembled community. No mercy must be shown. Sneers hiss like sharp arrows to and fro. Weaknesses and faults and lies are uncovered with wit and edged laughter. But behind all such castigation, says Knud Rasmussen, there must be a touch of humor, for mere abuse in itself is barren and cannot bring about any reconciliation. It is legitimate to be nasty, but one must be amusing at the same time in order to make the audience laugh. For laughter cures.

Thalbitzer reports a similar custom as practiced among the Greenland Eskimo: the opponents give vent to their anger in a most poetical form, drumming and singing against each other until all anger is evaporated and peace has been established among the enemies.

Thus the contest songs of the Eskimo (and one finds the same custom among African tribes) may well be classified under the Songs of Healing, for they heal a soul stifled with hidden anger and poisoned by baneful repression. By giving an outlet to pent-up aggres-

sion and animosity, the twisted mind is straightened
out, cleansed and renewed.

As a means of keeping up the sound equilibrium
both of individual and of group, the art of poetry
stands foremost among the natives of the Americas.
Nothing worse, in fact, can be laid upon the heart of
the Eskimo than the consciousness of being denied the
gift of singing. Among the Amassalik Eskimo a tra-
dition is handed down of a woman who went through
life without ever having been able to sing a song. A
most lamentable fate! After her death, an *angaqok* had
to undertake one of his professional journeys to the
spirit land. Having arrived there, he met the woman
—just happily singing a song. Down he rushed to tell
the mourning husband about the fortunate transfor-
mation. He indeed could receive no better news; with
beaming eyes, he sprang up and whirled around in
jubilation. Death, then, was not so bad after all when
it could transform a most unfortunate person into a
perfectly happy one!

SONGS OF GROWTH AND GERMINATION

In a way, the songs of growth and germination may
also be grouped in the class of healing songs. It is with
these songs of growing and maturing that the Indian
reveals most conspicuously his innermost being—his
integral relationship to the forces of nature and the
universe.

The Indian of the Southwest, for instance, after
having planted the seeds of his corn, sings softly at
eventide the ancient tunes, while he is pounding the

earth with his feet and the drum is throbbing in the rhythm of his blood and of all things growing—perhaps a song as recorded by Ruth Underhill among the Papago Indians of Arizona:

> Blue evening falls,
> Blue evening falls,
> Near by, in every direction.
> It sets the corn tassels trembling.

The Indian becomes part of the creative divinity that lives in all things germinating and unfolding. Streams of renewal—welling up from the powers below, pouring down from the powers above—are flooding his being and are doubled in strength within himself, and he returns it in chanted word and gesture of solemn summoning. The Indian thus experiences himself as an active part of the creative processes of the earth, which are forever progressing and retarding, swelling and subsiding, in the gigantic rhythm of the cosmos.

While the Indian, during the times of general maturing, abandons his personality and flings all of his spiritual power into the caldron of renewal, he himself will be renewed. While he joins the supernatural forces in the annually recurring process of creation, he himself will be recreated and made over from the bottom of his being. The words that are believed to promote fertility, fructify not only the soil that has received the seed of the corn, but also the soil of his soul.

To have once witnessed a religious ceremony—for instance, the Corn Dance as performed so superbly by the Santo Domingo Indians of New Mexico—helps one to understand better than anything else the Indians relation to the word as the powerful agency that brings about what he desires most—that is, germination, growth, fertility.

Though with some Indian tribes, as we have seen, song was not quite unknown as a means of spontaneous self-expression and was not infrequently composed on the spur of the moment, on the whole the song of the American Indian can fully be understood only in its functional setting, as a product and tool of the group and deep-rooted tradition. Only if it is heard as part of a ceremony, be it one of purification, curing, or initiation, does one become quite aware of the intensely pragmatic function of all song. And even though one may not understand the language proper, it is possible to feel the meaning of a song if heard as part of its spiritual matrix, against the background of native culture and native landscape.

It was a hot day in August. The highway leading to the pueblo was an avenue flanked by tall sunflowers —and beyond this brilliant hedge of ever so many sun-disks the desert stretched, dotted with sagebrush, to the purple ranges of distant mountains, slope after slope, until they were lost in the haze of the heat-misted skies.

When we arrived, the Saint had already been carried to his bower of evergreen branches, and women had placed their offerings of bread and fruit before the image. A group of *Koshairi* were just emerging from the Turquoise Kiva, and the dancers were moving from the cottonwoods, near the church, toward the sun-parched plaza.

A drum was sounding—as it seemed from nowhere. Rattles were rapping, feet were pounding, voices united in a chant. The second part of the dance had begun. One's own soul seemed to respond almost immediately to the sudden up-surge of powers which live in everyone, powers that are only the condensed expression of man's yearning for growth and the gentle unfolding of that which is hidden and yet brimful with life. One's very being seemed to be woven instantly into the rich pattern of drumbeat, song, rattle chime, thudding of moccasined feet—and the indescribably delicate gestures of mute prayer.

Behind the men, the women moved. The men—urgent, powerful, insistent. The women—rapt, self-abandoned, and yet exquisitely self-restrained. On their heads the women wore the green *tablitas,* carved prayers for clouds and rain. The black ceremonial garment contrasted strikingly with the brown skin of bare shoulders and bare arms; into their red sashes twigs of spruce were tucked, and they held a bunch of spruce in each hand, moving them up and down in the rhythm of the dance. The sky was blue and the sand of the plaza red hot. The women danced barefoot. They followed the men, who, like the women, had their hair flowing. But they had fastened in it feathers of the parrot, for men, it is said, are closer to the powers above. The men did not dance barefoot. Their feet were securely moccasined, their ankles edged with fur of the skunk; and while they pranced, the fox pelt, fastened at the back of their white Hopi kilt, dangled and whipped and wagged, touching at times the women. With the right hand they shook the blackened gourd rattle, and in the left they carried the symbol of life, the spruce. Spruce everywhere—it sprouted out of their belts, their bracelets, out of the vividly colored worsted garters and the strings of hoof-rattles and bells beneath their knees. On the bare breast some wore an abalone shell, some a few strings of turquoise, and others only a single arrowpoint.

And in and out, through the varying formations of the dance, the *Koshairi* moved, the spirits of the dead, controlling and blessing the ways of the living, expressing to perfection the essence of all Pueblo religion: the creative coalition between the intangible realities of what we call the Other World and the palpable phenomena of the Here and Now. With the Puebleños there is no gap between these two systems of experience. The dead dance with the living. It seems to be difficult, however, to make sure whether the *Koshairi* are believed really to represent the spirits of the dead or whether they are only related to them in some mysterious way, and therefore merely assist the *shiwanni*—that is, the cloud-beings—in their attempts at fertilizing the earth. However, their make-up indicated clearly their close association with death. Their bodies were painted a grayish white, the color of decay and decomposition. Black stripes here and there across the chest and around the eyes intensified the impression that we were watching beings which had just emerged from the underworld. Their hair, plastered with clay, was done up in two horns of cornhusk, which also stand for death.

I did not notice any clowning.[7] Serenely they danced

[7] The spirits of the dead, while they join the living during certain ceremonies in the pueblos, have to fulfill various functions. They are supposed to promote not only general fertility and to bless the maturing crops, but also to punish certain individuals by ridiculing them. "Clownish" actions, seemingly amusing, have quite frequently an "educational" purpose.

their individual patterns, individual yet in perfect rhythm with the group of the living. Exquisite were their gentle gestures of blessing, graceful their pantomimes of coercive summoning.

And ever in response to drumbeat and song the intensity of the dance was swelling with soft insistence and subsiding again like the tides of the sea.

We had climbed meantime to the roof of a two-storied house where we could look down upon the long lines of the dancers as well as upon the chorus of old men. This change of position threw into high relief the fact that the directing power of the ceremony was actually radiated from this group of singing men: it was the chanted word that ensouled the dance and integrated its various patterns, both the unfettered moves of the "dead" and the rigidly prescribed steps of the "living," into the perfection of a highly elaborated work of art.

There was no difficulty in understanding the meaning of the song as sung by these old men. Out of the depths of their souls they called for growth and abundance. And their song was a prayer, a danced prayer, as it were; for while they sang they performed a sort of posture dance. Like a flower that unfolds and closes its petals, they raised their arms and turned their faces upward imploringly, only to withdraw again for short intervals into the sheltering circle of their ceremonial isolation, to gather new spiritual strength, it seemed. The strength that emanated from the singing men had an almost material quality. They radiated this power to the dancers, who translated it into step and gesture; thus they conveyed it more effectively to the outside powers which live under the skies and in the darkness of the earth.

Here again the twofold function of all song became most conspicuous. It was obvious that the men, in singing the song, first gained power for themselves. Only then did it serve to enhance the power of all those phenomena in the outside world whose purpose it is to induce germination and to hasten growth.

Still another example shows the creative potency which the Indian believes to live in the word.

The more war-loving Chippewa of the northern woodlands developed during the painful period of transition a strange custom, extremely interesting from a psychotherapeutical point of view.[8]

It was the practice among the Chippewa—as also among most of the Plains tribes—for the youth who stood at the threshold of manhood to go out into solitude, fasting four days in silence and reverence, in preparation for a vision that would determine his future life. In this vision he would receive a song that he would sing only when he was about to enter the most decisive moment of his life: his first encounter with a foe. The arrival of the white man and the enforced and too monotonously peaceful life on a reservation made going on the warpath, by and by, a custom of the past. Thus, the song formerly received in a dream vision remained unsung.

But this song meant a reservoir of power, of unused magic and strength. And unused energy—every psychiatrist knows it—is a constant threat to the mental

[8] See Frances Densmore, *Chippewa Music, II*. Bureau of American Ethnology, *Bulletin* 53 (1913), pp. 247-50.

equilibrium of a person who carries with him, as in the case of the Chippewa—the secretly working and ever-urging force of an unfulfilled dream. The Chippewa, in order to avert the threat of being slowly destroyed by his own "power," erects a pole. On top of it he fastens a rag on which he has painted the symbols of his song—the sun, the moon, a star, or a deer. And everybody will know that in the hut in front of which stands such a pole lives a man who never sang his song, but who has the magic power to heal and to fight the fiercest of all enemies, death. He has transferred the energy which cannot find an outlet in the accustomed way into another field of activity.

In parenthesis it may be added that the problem which these "primitives" were facing and solving according to their own needs and their own standards is not so very different from the psychological issue of our time and our own culture. Our crumbling ideals and values, our wobbling beliefs and anemic convictions seem to have got stuck in a "reservation" of utter dullness, and our longings and hopes lead a pitiful existence of spiritual starvation. We are beset with a perpetually gnawing consciousness of unfulfillment, even though it may be felt only vaguely by most of us. Unused energy is threatening to eat us up from within, and it is a major task of our own "medicine men of the soul" to give these undirected energies a new and meaningful direction. The passionate culture criticism of an R. M. Holzapfel or an Edward Sapir has not yet lost its poignant validity, unfortunately.

SILENCE, SOLITUDE, AND THE SECRET

I cannot conclude this chapter on the word and its magic healing power, as experienced by the aborigines of America, without mentioning his relation to the creative potency that is inherent in silence, the secret, and solitude.

Wherever the word is revered as a tool around which still vibrates the magic halo of primeval creation, there silence, too, is esteemed a reservoir of spiritual strength. Wherever the value of the word deteriorated, turning into a cheap weapon and an easy coin, the intrinsic meaning of silence was also lost. We, indeed, live in a period of an alarming inflation of the word, and nothing is more symptomatic of it than our aversion to silence and quietude that amounts to phobia. A mother of our civilization is deeply worried when her child prefers the ways of solitude and reticent seclusion.

The attitude of the Indian toward the various forms of solitude and silence is altogether different, and the education in quietude and reticence are crucial parts of the child's training.

Says the Lakota Indian Chief, Standing Bear:

Training began with children who were taught to sit still and enjoy it. They were taught to use their organs of smell, to look when there was apparently nothing to see, and to listen intently when all seemingly was quiet. A child that cannot sit still is a half-developed child.

And again:

Excessive manners were put down as insincere, and the constant talker was considered rude and thoughtless. Conversation was never begun at once, nor in a hurried manner. No one was quick with a question, no matter how important, and no one was pressed for an answer. A pause giving time for thought was the truly courteous way of beginning and conducting a conversation. Silence was meaningful with the Dakota. . . . Also in the midst of sorrow, sickness, and death, or misfortune of any kind, and in the presence of the notable and great, silence was the mark of respect. More powerful than words was silence with the Lakota. . . .

The esteem in which silence was held goes hand in hand with a preference for moderation in all ways. To raise the voice was considered a mark of inferiority. Said Maria Chona, a Papago woman, to Ruth Underhill:

My father went on talking to me in a low voice. That is how our people always talk to their children, so low and quiet, the child thinks he is dreaming. But he never forgets.

The merciless abuse of the word on the part of the white man was, it seems, already current at the time when the Jesuit Fathers set out to do missionary work among the red men. For when Paul Le Jeune jotted down the first impressions the Indians had made upon him, he emphasized as the most striking one the fact "that they do not all talk at once, but one after the other, listening patiently." And it was for this very reason that he preferred to share a cabin with the "primitives" rather than with his own countrymen, who could not keep quiet for a minute.

One of the reasons why modern man, generally speaking, avoids the silence of solitude and meditation with such circumspection, is that he fears to face the emptiness of his world. He rather drugs himself with the opiates of noise, speed, and bustle, which render him immune against the giddying sight of this yawning emptiness which is his heaven and his soul.

But to the Indian there was no such thing as emptiness in the world. There was no object around him that was not alive with spirit, and earth and tree and stone and the wide scope of the heaven were tenanted with numberless supernaturals and the wandering souls of the dead. And it was only in the solitude of remote places and in the sheltering silence of the night that the voices of these spirits might be heard.

Ohiyesa lamented deeply the loss of solitude with which the Indian was afflicted with the advance of the white man's noisy civilization. Says he in his fine book, *The Soul of the Indian:*

To the untutored sage the concentration of population was the prolific mother of all evils, moral no less than physical. . . . And not less dreaded than the pestilence following upon crowded and unsanitary dwellings was the loss of spiritual power inseparable from too close contact with one's fellow men. All who have lived much out of doors know that there is a magnetic and nervous force that accumulates in solitude and that is quickly dissipated by life in a crowd.

Another Plains Indian, also of high standing, Black Elk, suffering immeasurably from having to watch helplessly his people's rapid decline, went across the Big Water to the homelands of the white man, in the vain hope of learning ways with which to mend the broken hoop of his nation. He returned, stunned from the din and smoke and narrowness of crowded cities. And he felt, characteristically, like a man who could never dream a dream again.

Owing to his infallible religious instinct, the Indian not only made the observation of silence and long

41

vigils of solitude important parts of his childrens' and his own training but, being fully aware of the role which the "secret" plays in the religious development of the individual, he taught his children strict reticence about the most decisive experiences they had during their initiatory rites.

Many of the Western psychiatrists, living, just as their patients do, under the general spell of word inflation, have made it a point of their therapy to mark any individual secret as a serious obstacle to the recovery of the lost mental balance. Hence the vogue of endless "confessions" and alarming self-analyses.

The Indian, however, discriminated soundly between the soul-endangering influence of the secret an evil deed could exert and the healing power of a religious secret. Only the former had to be confessed in the face of the community, lest the owner of this secret be destroyed by the poison it was capable of spreading; the latter was treasured as the most precious personal possession of the individual. The Omaha youth never tells of the vision he receives during the rites of adolescence. And likewise the Yuma Indian says that if a "man tells his dream, it passes with the day." And among the Wishram, "no one ever revealed how he came by his spirit; only at the hour of death he disclosed all the mysteries pertaining to it." And, continues Dr. Spier, even those Indians who seem thoroughly civilized and sophisticated guard their spirit-power which they received in a dream as a secret and tell it to no one. Clark Wissler also, in his unexcelled classics on the Blackfoot Indians, points out repeatedly the importance of the religious secret in the individual development of members of this northern Plains tribe.

It seems, indeed, a sign of cultural maturity rather than of pubescence when not only the word is considered sacred and is therefore used with reverent economy, but when also the individual "secret" is esteemed sacred as an inalienable personal possession.

SONGS OF VISION AND OF DREAM

Songs might be obtained in two different ways. One method cultivated by the Indians of the plains is the following: a youth or a man who is troubled with grief he no longer can bear without supernatural help goes out into the solitude to seek a vision in which Wakonda may reveal himself and bestow upon him a song that will guide him throughout his future life. Severe fasting and long vigils are absolutely necessary prerequisites for the acquisition of supernatural help, which is by no means always granted.[9]

Another way is practiced by various tribes of southern California and the southwestern deserts, the Yuma and Mohave especially. The power of the song comes to them unsought in the dream of the night, though there are exceptions where the song-bestowing dream is artificially produced by means of a drug, jimsonweed. But the natives themselves admit that the days of those who try to direct spiritual power upon themselves in this manner are numbered.

These southwestern desert tribes are of a curious

[9] Ruth Benedict, "The Vision in Plains Culture," in *American Anthropologist*, New Series, XXIV.

interest from a psychological point of view. Though they are neighbors of the Pueblo people, who are given to rigid ritual and ceremony, outward expressions of religious life have little or no appeal to them.

They are in need neither of priesthood nor of altar; symbol, mask, and formalized prayer find no place in their religious practices. For with these tribes, the dream is the only source and evidence of supernatural power, and everybody might be a medicine man or priest according to his dreams. Says Leslie Spier, to whom we are indebted for some of the most elucidating accounts and analyses of those tribes who have made the dream the center around which all the activities of their daily routine circle:

> At the heart of the Maricopa culture was the dream experience. It was the one thing of which they constantly talked, the significant aspect of their life as they saw it. . . . Dream experience was at the bottom of all success in life, and as such their constant preoccupation. Learning was displaced by dreaming. . . . A single statement of Last Star's epitomizes their attitude: "Everyone who is prosperous or successful must have dreamed of something. It is not because he is a good worker that he is prosperous, but because he dreamt."

Moreover, the individual dream is not only the basis of every success and achievement whatsoever, but also of shamanistic power, of myth and song and supernatural relations. All myths and songs, though in reality handed down by ancient tradition, are dreamed anew by each narrator and singer.

Needless to say, the songs obtained thus in dreams conform to a definite pattern of the tribal culture and only seldom deviate considerably from the grooves chiseled out by the dream experiences of generations.

44

This fact, however, does not impair a sense of individual creativeness so characteristic of these people: everybody is sure to shape his life according to his dreams in perfect freedom from tradition, just as the Pueblo potter is convinced that the designs she has dreamed about are new creations of her mind and not merely repetitions of ancient patterns. In any case, a dream is obliging, and it is a strict requirement that a medicine man must live up to his dream; else his power will depart, and his life will be shortened.

The Jesuit Fathers were keen observers and born anthropologists. It is thus of interest to read Father François Du Peron's letter on the Hurons in reference to the paramount role the dream played in the life of these northern tribes. Says he:

All their actions are dictated to them directly by the devil, who speaks to them now in the form of a crow or some similar bird, now in the form of a flame or a ghost, and all this in dreams, to which they show great deference. They consider the dream as the master of their lives, it is the God of the country. It is this which dictates to them their feasts, their hunting, their fishing, their war, their trade with the French, their remedies, their dances, their games, their songs.

The words of these dream songs are usually obscure, as it is their purpose to conceal the true meaning of the dream to the outsider. But to the owner every word is fraught with spiritual potency and significance. These words are his fetish, his shield, and his never-failing source of renewal. Above all, his song is instrumental in re-establishing in the hour of need the condition under which it came to him—a condition of direct communication with deity.

The Plains Indian not only tries to prepare himself for a vision by seeking the solitude of nature, undisturbed by man, and by the endurance of hunger and sorrowful vigils during long nights of loneliness, but he also aims to make his subconscious susceptible to the helping influences of the supernaturals by the steady contemplation of certain aspects of nature, until he gradually loses the sense of his own personality and identifies himself with the forms of his environment. In his growing trance he becomes so very much part of the tree, the storm, the thunder, the animal which he contemplates, that when finally the song comes to him it is the song of the thunder or of the tree that he is learning and making his own.

We choose two examples from Frances Densmore's work on the Chippewa. The words of the first song are:

The wind only I am afraid of.

And the words of the other:

Sometimes
I go about pitying myself
While I am carried by the wind
Across the sky.

The exact meaning of these songs could not be understood if it were not for the explanation the interpreter gave Miss Densmore.

The first song was received by a youth during a vision in which he heard the trees singing as though they were alive. They sang that they feared nothing but the wind, for only the winds could defeat them. After this vision the young man identified himself with the trees, for he will be afraid of nothing on his warpath;

46

of nothing but the howling winds—and these will never crush him.

The second song echoed out of the contemplation of the storm mystery, out of the sky and the immense loneliness of the prairie. The dreamer becomes the companion of the swirling winds beneath the sky—torn away from his tribesmen, and therefore suffering, but close to the place where the powers dwell.

SONG AND DEATH

The Lakota Chief Standing Bear says in his fine *Autobiography:*

Sometimes during the night or stillness of day, a voice would be heard singing the brave song. This meant that sorrow was present—either a brave was going on the warpath and expected to die, or else a family was looking for the death of some member of it. *The brave song was to fortify one to meet any ordeal bravely and to keep up faltering spirits.* I remember, when we children were on our way to Carlisle School, thinking that we were on our way to meet death at the hands of the white people, the older boys sang brave songs, so that we would all meet death according to the code of the Lakota—fearlessly.

It is this custom of the brave song—or death song—in which the Indian soul expresses itself at its purest; a custom, as it seems, unknown among other people, so far as I am aware; with the one exception of the Japanese, perhaps.

Among scholars little attention has been paid as yet to this noble custom we find scattered here and there among various tribes of the American Indian. Some authorities seem to doubt altogether whether there existed a song type that could be called a true death song. But there is hardly any autobiography written by an Indian that does not at least mention its existence. The Jesuit Fathers, brave and indomitable explorers of the Indian mind, likewise mention frequently the death song as practiced among the tribes of the Iroquois, the Ottawa, and the Huron.

Due to the lack of any thorough investigation into this matter, there is no way of saying whether the custom of singing a death song in the moment of utmost danger or in the very hour of dissolution was restricted to certain areas or distributed all over the continent. This much is sure—the Indians of the Plains as well as those of the northwest coast and the southwestern deserts were well familiar with it.

Material shows that there existed two different patterns of the death song. The one resembles essentially the dream song, for it is received during a vision or a dream, but it is to be sung only in an hour of utter desolation, or when death stands face to face with the individual. The second type, however, is composed in the very hour of death and chanted with the last breath of the dying man.

As an example of the former class, a song heard by Dr. Lowie among the Crow Indians may follow:

> Eternal are the heavens and the earth;
> Old people are poorly off.
> Do not be afraid.

A few casual words, it may seem. Yet they comprise the essence of a world view, grim but serene: absence of a consoling belief in the continuance of man's soul after death, yet calm acceptance of the inevitable; and the assurance that it is better to die young amid the din of the battle, for it is a pitiful thing to be old and decrepit.

The songs of the second order reflect, at times most vividly, the stress of the hour, great suffering and great self-control.

It is again to Frances Densmore that we turn for a suitable example from her vast collection of Indian songs and lore, unfortunately somewhat difficult of access for the ordinary reader.

She tells the story of Namébinés, a leading warrior of the Chippewa, who was badly wounded during a fight with the Sioux. At his own request his comrades, who were about to retreat, laid him near the sheltering bushes to die. With his last strength he sang his death song he had composed at this time:

> The odor of death,
> I discern the odor of death
> In front of my body.

And, looking into the faces of his friends, he added: "When you reach home sing this song for the women to dance by and tell them how I died. . . ."

There is something of Greek grandeur and Greek simplicity about the dying of this wounded Indian, high up in the northern woods of America. His words of departure seem like a faint echo of those words engraved upon the tombstone of the warriors fallen at Thermophylae ages ago.

And here is the last song of a man who was about to be hanged, also composed on the spur of the moment:

> They will take me home,
> The spirits.

49

And the death song of a warrior, left behind on the deserted battlefield and assisted only by his friend:

> From the middle
> Of the great water
> I am called by the spirits.

Light as the last breath of the dying, these words flutter out and seem to mingle with the soft fumes and mists that rise from the river in the morning. It is as though the song, with the lightness of a bird's feather, will carry the departing soul up to where the stars are glittering and yonder where the rainbow touches the dome of the sky.

In the mind of the Indian, song is associated with death in many ways.

All over the world we meet with the belief that whatever is valued most highly among a people is connected in some way or other with the dead. Thus the Pueblo Indians assume that song, way back in times primeval, ascended from the realm of the dead and to this day has its roots down in the nourishing soil of Shipap.

The snake in North American mythology is usually associated not only with sky and water, rainbow, stars, and lightning, but also with the powers of the underworld, with night, destruction, and renewal. The serpent is conceived as a power that rules life as well as death.

The origin myth of the southern Diegueño, for instance, tells how song came into being.[10] After

[10] Leslie Spier, *Southern Diegueño Customs,* University of California Publications in American Archaelogy and Ethnology, Berkeley, 1923, pp. 328 *et seq.*

Tcikumat, the creator, had died, Wild Cat took charge of the cremation ceremonies. He ordered an enclosure to be built of wood, then he sent for Mattiawít, the mythical snake. He came. And he coiled his length around the pyre upon which the remains of the god were to be burned. Then fire was set to the structure. The serpent, amid the leaping flames, burst asunder— "part flew back to the place he had come from, the rest burst into fragments. Each piece that flew off to the people was a song. Each gens received a song. . . ."

The serpent had come from the underworld, the realm of death, and, dying, he created song for man.

In the life of the Eskimo, song, as we have seen, played a paramount role. According to Knud Rasmussen, not only the name of the drum with which they accompany the song, *quilaut,* is related to *quilwsk,* which means "the art of getting in touch with the spirits," but song itself is firmly believed to have come from the souls in the land of the dead.[11]

Among the Omahas of the Plains there exists an interesting funeral custom. When a woman or a man greatly loved and respected dies, the young men of the camp meet where the dead lies. Each of the youths makes two incisions in his upper left arm, and under the loop of the flesh thrusts a small willow twig. With the blood dripping on the leaves of the sprays, the men move in single file, facing the tent of the departed.

The contrast between the bleeding singers [says Alice Fletcher, the authority on the Omaha Indians] and the blithe major cadences of the song, suggestive of birds, sun-

[11] Knud Rasmussen, *The Intellectual Culture of the Iglulik Eskimo,* Copenhagen, 1929, pp. 228-9.

shine, and the delights of the upper air, throws light on the Omaha belief relative to death and to song. Music, it was explained, can reach the unseen world and carry thither man's thought and aspirations. The song is of the spirit of the dead; it is to cheer him as he goes from his dear ones left behind on earth; so, as he hears the voices of his friends, their glad tones help him to go forward on his inevitable journey.

Among the Winnebago of the Great Lakes district, the Picuris Indians of the Southwest, and the Tlingit of the northwest coast, it was the custom to sing songs to bridge for the departed the long and fearful distance that stretches between the land of the living and the land of the dead.

Chapter II: The Influence of Christianity Upon the Aboriginal Cultures of America

In this collection of indigenous prose and poetry there is hardly a passage or a verse which is not faintly touched by the white man's influence, if only by passing through the medium of a foreign language. Even those examples chosen from biographies written and translated by natives themselves can only be understood against the background of transition and as the results of the tragic clash of two cultures which could, as yet, neither be fused nor welded into a new creative whole.

Many of the items of this anthology, then, represent vividly a state of transition and assimilation, or are the expression of dogged defense and passionate rejection, as the case may be. This, in my opinion, does not affect the value of the material. On the contrary, from a psychological point of view, its significance cannot well be underrated. The individual who, in the hour of smarting change and in the face of foreign ideas and bewildering new ways of life, gives vent to his sentiments and thoughts will perhaps allow a deeper insight into the hidden recesses of his soul than he does in tale and speech and song produced in times of sheltered and undisturbed tradition.

Besides, Ohiyesa's pessimism as to the dubious value of the hitherto garnered myths and songs is valid only as far as the Plains Indians are concerned, and even then only to a certain degree. This brilliant race indeed succumbed utterly to the devastating influence of alien doctrines, of trade, whisky, spirit of competition, and pitiful misunderstanding. But to most of the remaining tribes can be applied—with some minor modifications—what Cushing said of the Zuñi Indians:

> The Zuñi faith . . . is a drop of oil in water, surrounded and touched at every point, yet in no place penetrated or changed inwardly by the flood of alien belief that descended upon it. . . . The Zuñi adjusts other beliefs and opinions to his own, but never his own beliefs and opinions to others; and even his usages are almost never changed in spirit, however much so in externals. . . . Thus he is slow to adopt from alien people any but material suggestions . . . and especially in religious culture, the Zuñi is almost as strictly archaic as in the days ere his land was discovered.

Still, the problem in which the student of cultural contacts is most interested, is not only the question of what attracted the native and which of the culture elements he selected, but also how he assimilated the adopted elements and, above all, which of the new ideas he instinctively refused to accept.

Ohiyesa stresses the fact that there was undoubtedly much in primitive Christianity to appeal to the Indian. Above all, it was the ritual of baptism that was likely to bridge the old familiar traditions with the new belief which the zealous missionaries tried to graft upon the bewildered minds of the Indians.

The Jesuit Father Allouez, who worked among the Ottawa tribes, remarked in his journal (1666) that eventually the "savages" had lost their dread of baptism as causing death; they were now beginning to see in this rite a means of curing sickness and raising

54

up the dying. Some thirty years previous to the experiences of Father Allouez, Paul Le Jeune comments in his usual drastic and lively manner on the matters of baptism, using a report of Father Brébeuf. Says he:

Some Savages have become Christians this year; three have been baptized this winter during my absence. The first was a young man named Sasoumat. Father Brébeuf gave me this account of him.

"Having learned of the illness of this young man, I went to visit him, and, having sounded him, we found him filled with a great desire to receive Holy Baptism. We deferred this for a few days, in order to instruct him more fully. At last he sent word to me, through our savage Manitougatche, that I should come and baptize him, saying that the night before he had seen me in his sleep, coming to his cabin to administer to him this sacrament; and that, as soon as I sat down near him, all his sickness went away. . . . Nevertheless I refused his request, in order the more to stimulate his desire, so that another savage who was present, not being able to bear this delay, asked me why I did not baptize him, since it was only necessary to throw a little water upon him."

Good medicine meant baptism to the Indians of the Woods, and the tangible components of this sacrament seemed familiar and thus convincing.

The same Fathers who understood so well how to win the hearts of the natives with the life-preserving magic of baptism had less success with the Last Sacrament and the doctrine of hell. Elsie C. Parsons is quite right when she says, referring to the Zapotec Indians of Mexico, that if the Church could have presented the last sacrament as supplying medicine for the last journey, this rite would have taken root.

But seldom could the Indians accept the idea of reward and punishment after death, much though the early missionaries operated with the concept to make the souls of the poor heathen more pliable. Most of the Indians held the concept of hell in contempt and thought it downright barbarous. For instance, in the pantheon of the Acoma Indians, the Christian Dios—Yoshti—maintains his place side by side with the sun god, the spirits of the dead, the revered clouds, the twin war gods, and the moon. But he is not regarded as very powerful, and he is not held in great respect, for, as a native puts it, "he is not particularly well disposed toward the people, and he punishes some people after death; none of our deities do this." The first place in the divine hierarchy—after a long and persistent contact with the Catholic Church—is still occupied by Jaticu, the benign mother who resides at Shipap, the place whence all life emerges and to which it again returns. She is most sacred, she does not punish, and a tender feeling is kept for her. The presence of her breath is felt wherever a prayer is spoken and a sacrifice offered.[1]

In many places, Jesus and the Virgin have found a way into the hearts of the aborigines, but they are seldom believed to exert any control over the most important things in the lives of the natives—namely, over the fertility of the soil, rain and sunshine, and the growth of the crops. Still, they are accepted as successful curers and have, according to experience, worked as well as many of the aboriginal charms and fetishes.

"Curing-methods of all kinds," says Parsons in her book on Mitla, "from calling stray spirits, chasing off

[1] Leslie A. White, *The Acoma Indians*, 47th Report of the Bureau of American Ethnology, 1929/30.

evil spirits down to sucking . . . are absolutely in accord with the Church."

The catholicized Indian has little use for the devil, for if he wants to do harm to some enemy, all he has to do is to visit the three crosses of Calvary and pray sincerely to the saints at noontime. For it is the saints who work for good and for evil. Thus, while San Antonio del Mundo at Mitla is the patron saint of the curers, San Esquipula is the secret helper of those who wish to inflict an ailment upon some disliked person.

The saints simply turned into local spirits—that is into supernaturals who are capable of bringing about sickness and death upon urgent request as well as being able to heal and to raise the dead.

Various tribes, though, took readily enough to Christian concepts and symbols—provided they promised to be the vehicles of greater power. Christ was said to heal the sick and to make the blind see. Naturally, Indians stricken with trachoma welcomed the new Transformer with understandable enthusiasm.

An autobiographical note of the Oglala Sioux, Sword, is of interest in this connection. Says he:

In war with the white people I found their Wakan Tanka superior. I then . . . served Wakan Tanka according to the white people's manner and with all my power.

However, he continued to treasure his shamanistic bundle—the *wasicun*—and, thus he frankly admits, he was "afraid to offend it, because the spirit of an Oglala may go to the spirit land of the Lakota." [2]

Other tribes again accepted and assimilated Christian concepts more willingly than other tribes on ac-

[2] J. R. Walker, *The Sun Dance and Other Ceremonies of the Oglala Division of the Teton Dakota*, 1917, p. 159.

count of a certain doctrinal similarity between the native religion and the new belief. Dr. Spier has shown that the Ghost Dance religion of 1890, hitherto considered as having sprung up mainly under the influence of, and as a reaction against, Christian influences, had its historical antecedent in the Prophet Dance of the Northwest, the doctrine of which "belief in the impending destruction and renewal of the world, when the dead would return" was aboriginal.

On the whole, Christianity only seldom touches the deepest core of the indigenous religious life, in spite of intense missionary work. This is shown impressively by the study of J. Eric Thompson in the religious practices of the Maya of Southern and British Honduras. The life of these Maya-speaking people of San Antonio, originally emigrants from San Luis in Peten, centers round agriculture, and all their thoughts and emotions are rooted in their soil and are bound up with sowing and with harvesting. The *milpa* is their home and their temple and their altar; it is there that they meet God, and the angels, and the ancient deities. It is only in connection with the preparation of the *milpa*, though, that the prayers to the old lords of field and forest have survived. Even the memory of the feathered serpent has faded, and the esoteric anthropomorphization of mathematical concepts has left no trace on the minds of these tillers of the soil. But the old agricultural deities still guard the *milpa*; and the Chacs— that is, the rain gods and the spirits of the dead—still hover around the maturing crops; the lords of the forest have not yet vanished.

The Socotz Maya, before clearing the *milpa*, erects an altar on the field, with calabashes as drink offerings to the gods. Previous to cutting the first tree, a lump of copal is burned, and while the fumes of the incense ascend, the Maya recites the following prayer:

O God, my mother, my father, Huitz-Hok, Lord of the Hills and Valleys, Che, Spirit of the Forests, be patient with me, I am about to do as my fathers have ever done. Now I make my offering to you as I am about to trouble your soul. You will perhaps have the strength to suffer it. I am about to dirty you, I am going to work you in order that I may live. I pray you suffer no snake to bite me. Permit not the scorpion or the wasp to sting me. Bid the trees that they fall not upon me, with all my soul I am going to work you.

During sowing time similar prayers are spoken, and at the season when rain is needed, the rain deities are addressed and offerings are made. If the prayers for rain are not answered in the expected way, the natives turn to the saints of the Church and call their attention to the drought menacing the crops. If this, too, is not effective, any saint is taken outside and placed right in the parching sun, so that he or she may know how it feels.

One should be surprised, says J. Eric Thompson, not that so little but rather that so much has survived of the ancient religion.

. . . despite three centuries of cruel tyranny, cold-blooded abuse, and heartless persecution by both the civil and religious authorities . . . the atrocities committed on the natives of Latin America during these three centuries have revealed the Christian civilization in no bright light. In Yucatán, only since the introduction of the semisocialist regime has the Maya been treated as a human being rather than a beast of burden. The Maya is no longer whipped for not attending or being late for church. . . .

I think we have overemphasized the Indian's clinging to tradition, his stubborn obduracy to change. There is ample evidence that aborigines received missionaries with the utmost courtesy, eager to hear the message of the Great Shining Spirit from across the Big Water. The way the Illinois received Father Marquette on his route down the Mississippi is one example of how the "savages" willingly opened their ears to the story of the unknown god. Simple and beautiful is the speech with which the Chief answered the address of Father Marquette and worth quoting here:

I thank thee, Black Gown, and thee, Frenchman, [turning to Joliet] for having taken so much trouble to come to visit us. Never has the earth been so beautiful, as today; never has our river been so calm, or so clear of rocks, which your canoes have removed in passing; never has our tobacco tasted so good, or our corn appeared so fine, as we now see them . . . I beg thee to have pity on me and on all my nation. It is thou who knowest the Great Spirit who has made us all. It is thou who speakest to Him, and who hearest His word. Beg Him to give me health and life and to come and dwell with us, in order to make us know Him.

These Illinois Indians, so sympathetically described by Father Marquette, are not an exception. The Nez Percé Indians even sent a delegation to St. Louis to ask for missionaries and the powerful Book of the white man. But wherever the native had the opportunity to gain a deeper insight into the teachings of Christianity and to watch at the same time the white man's way of living, he very soon became fully aware of the painful discrepancy between theory and practice. So the Indian closed himself away from the influences of a civilization that tolerated and even fostered treason, exploitation and cruelties without end.

THE INFLUENCE OF CHRISTIANITY

Don Diego de Vargas, the hero of the reconquest of New Mexico, and said to have been one of the most humane conquerors in the history of American colonization, summarizes his attitude toward the Indians in a letter to the Viceroy, as follows:

I have two aims and purposes in view, the first being the idea . . . to see if I can win them (the Indians) to our holy faith and, if so, have them as friends as in the case of the Taos tribe; and if unsuccessful in my purpose, and theirs is such that they persist rebellious and contumacious, then I will have them all destroyed and annihilated at once . . ."

What sort of response can be expected to a culture that offers a new creed on the point of a death-dealing sword? The many baptisms that followed in the wake of Vargas's reconquest were mostly not sincere.

It is in the Pueblo of Taos itself that one may observe most convincingly how Christianity touches as yet only the fringe of the native's inner world.

In the shadow of the two large terraced communal structures timidly hides the small missionary church. Its simple white cross gives the impression that it is trying to pull up the soul of the approaching worshiper, but the pull downward of the Kiva ladders, opposite, at the end of the plaza, seems to be stronger. The calls and signals to which the Indian responds still come from deep down, from out of the darkness where all things germinate and where the forces of life and death meet. The upward beck of the Cross has but little appeal to the Indian. His dead go down, not up.

Still, when we entered the little church on the day previous to the fiesta of San Geronimo to take part in the Vesper service which was being celebrated, we were absorbed immediately into an exquisite atmosphere of true devotion and sincere worship. There they were kneeling, the Indian women, wrapped in their colorful shawls, devout and yet casual, without strain or stress. They were given and opened to invisible influences; and their hands rested upon their children, who were sitting in front of them, playing noiselessly. Women kept coming and going, offering candles and lighting them at the base of the altar. Small Indian children squatted, lost in the sight of the lovely light that kept dancing and flickering, as if the breath of some unseen power were touching it all the time. The priest commenced intoning the old, time-holied cadences, and the choir was responding. The aged Indian, clad in the garments of his tribe, being the altar boy, swayed the incense vessel and made the silver bell ring. Divinity was present—who was not aware of it? But which divinity? Who knows the name of the god whose presence was felt in the hearts of the natives while the fumes of the incense was curling its fragrant way down the nave?

We left the church. The declining sun was steeping the mountain in an unearthly splendor of all tints of rose and purple, and the plaza was aglow in vibrant amber. The unaccented beat of a drum sounded muffled out of one of those subterranean kivas yonder. And when the sun was about to set, the old men emerged from the kiva and gathered in the front yard of the church. They were deeply blanketed, and each of them carried a branch of yellow aspen in his hands. And while the church bell was chiming, they began to chant their ancient prayers and to shuffle out of the yard, away from the Cross, along the rippling mountain stream, from pyramid to pyramid. And with song and dance they greeted the departing sun, it being the eve of his voyage through winter, death, and underworld. Out of the strength of their unitedness, out of the accumulated power that grows from the unity of rhythm and song and drum beat, the old men tried to bestow upon the failing sun the strength he might need on his perilous voyage. And while they sang words of magic and of power, they shuffled away from the Cross, always away, and even the memory of the Virgin's image seemed to have faded.

This trend became still more obvious during the ceremonies of the following day, the day of San Geronimo proper. The patron of the Pueblo sat within the bower of evergreen and aspen branches erected at the end of the ancient race track. Amid a crowd of visiting Apaches, Hopis, and Santo Domingo Indians, the Saint was watching benignly the races which were carried on not in a spirit of competition, but again in order to extend their strength to the Sun, who is about to encounter the dangerous powers of the underworld.[3]

The Puebleños were nude except for the breechcloth and the ceremonial kilt, the latter being beautifully embroidered with the images of the heavenly bodies and various symbols of growth and fertility. Their bodies were painted in many designs and glued all over with eagle down in order to gain the swiftness and the power of the wide-winged eagle.

I have seldom witnessed such joyful devotion, such concentrated and gladdened abandonment of self for

---

[3] Authorities seem to disagree as to the meaning of these races. The Indians are most reticent about such matters. But there is little doubt that the races are related to cosmic phenomena.

the benefit of a higher, though primitive, force. The onlooker, the gaping white man, no longer existed; he seemed to be obliterated. Only San Geronimo looked on. The Indians did not mind.

Thus, wherever the old spirit revives and the racial resources begin to flow again, the movement "back to the blanket" may be observed not infrequently, especially where indigenous religious concepts are concerned.

Leslie A. White was once told the dream of a native of Acoma. The content of this dream expresses exactly this retrospective attitude of many Indians of today. The man confessed that he had been certain all the time to disbelieve in the *Katcinas* (the spirits of the dead), Christ having replaced the spirits of the ancients. But then he dreamed he had died and gone to heaven. He found himself standing before God; he could not remember exactly how God looked, "but he seemed to resemble in appearance and dress a successful American businessman." He was in an officelike room, seated behind a desk, "just like a bank." God asked him, "Where is your license?" meaning, "Where is the sign that you have the right to enter heaven?" The Indian had a Bible and showed it. God said, "No. That's not your license." And he showed the man a prayer stick, saying that the Bible was the white man's license, but the prayer stick was the Indian's license.

All that this Indian, upon being questioned, had to reply was that the dream was right.

I do not doubt, however, that if the Indian of high standing had encountered really superior exponents of the Christian culture, capable of vivifying immortal beings like Augustine, Saint Francis, and Saint Theresa of Avila, the natives would have opened their hearts to the teachings of such a religion. For the Indian has a keen sense of what is true and genuine; he rejects only that which is spurious and false. But he was made to face Christianity at a time when its unity of faith with the demands of reality had fallen apart, when creed and life had begun to oppose each other, and, worst of all, when Western man, devoted to a life of action and not of contemplation, was beginning to make a virtue out of the tragic fact that he never could live up to his confessed ideal.

To the dubious attitude of the conqueror the Indian preferred his sheltering blanket, his old magic, and his primitive ideals.

CHRISTMAS AT SAN FELIPE

In many Pueblos of the American Southwest—at least where the aborigines have recovered the strength to withstand the more disintegrating influences of an alien civilization—the mission church has become an integral part not only of native architecture, but also of native life and religion. There appears to be no conflict between the emblems of the Christian church and the power-charged symbols of indigenous belief. The Chalice and the Immaculate Ear of Corn do not always exclude each other. Both stand for the unbroken flux of life. The Christian symbols which were thought to inspire an ascetic life, the ultimate goal of which was the Beyond, have not seldom received in the hands of the Indians their old pagan significance: they again serve the serious and joyful task of fructification of life in all its manifestations and the gentle but irresistible promotion of growth.

On the west bank of the Rio Grande, not far from one of those steep-cliffed mesas, the Pueblo of San Felipe lies. I spent only one night there—the night before Christmas. But it taught me more about Pueblo religion than many days spent in other Pueblos.

Midnight had already passed when our Indian friend led us from his house outside the court to the church. A misty rain hung in the air, and it was very silent. It was a relief to see, far distant, a window lighted; and though there was no star and no moon, the fortresslike church seemed to radiate a quaint light. The two massive towers with their open belfries stood out clearly against the velvety darkness of the night, and above the wooden gallery that connects the twin towers loomed the Cross, deepening still more the extreme severity of the architecture.

Inside, the priest was already celebrating the Mass. No Indian woman was kneeling, so far as I could see; here and there I noticed a man carrying a baby on his back, secured in the loop of the blanket slung around his body. The priest went slowly through the performance of his duties as the congregation looked on, standing about casually or kneeling. The priest mixed wine and water. He bent his head before the Tabernacle, praying. But there seemed to be no spreading sense of real devotion, no feeling of worship or of the presence of divinity. The priest appeared to be lost in his task, and, with his back turned toward the congregation most of the time, he seemed to have forgotten about the rest of humanity. The hour seemed long. It was uncomfortable, too, to kneel on the wet clay floor of the church with the rain steadily dropping through the roof all around.

Finally the priest departed. There was a moment in which it seemed as if life quickened all of a sudden, as if the dim lights of the church had acquired a new radiance. We lined up with the San Felipans to pay our tribute at the altar—to what I did not yet know. When I reached the sanctuario to give my little offering, I set eyes on the most unexpected sight of my life. María and José were lying in a bed on the altar, offerings of bread piled at their heads. The Indian in front of me was just lifting the bedcover gently and tucking it in again with solicitude and then kissing María, lightly, but with great devotion.

And this is why there is no conflict between the Christian doctrine and the native religion. Even María and José are made to serve the fulfillment of the one eternal desire of man, fertility, in whatever form it may be coveted.

Four or five little toy horses stood in line behind the bed, all of them looking down upon the couple with amazement, while a huge cow peeped around the corner of the altar, seeming shy and a little worried, as cows sometimes do. That the animals took such a lively part in the happenings of this Christmas Eve long, long ago is something which assuredly has an appeal to the Indian: there was a time, then, when man and animal, all around the earth, understood each other's language and were devoted fervently to each other's welfare.

Meantime, a strange silence had gathered in the church, charged with a peculiar power of an almost electric quality. And into this exciting quietude the voice of a bird fell, just a timid tinkle at first, a cautious call, but soon answered by innumerable voices of winged creatures, invisible and hidden away from the curious eye of man. There was a chirping and twittering without end, a gay chorus of birds announcing that there were things going to happen never seen before. . . .

The doors of the church were flung open. The dim thud of a drum was heard, the rhythmic beat of steps approaching—and out of the dark of the night the warriors emerged, filing into the church, stamping down the nave, whooping and rattling, and above this sudden din of voices, bells, shells, drums, the birds kept warbling and calling.

It was only with the second dance that I could understand—or at least I think I understood—the meaning of it all.

While the tenor of the first dance was a vivacious one, with much flaring red, flying eagle feathers, emphatic step, urgent song, powerful drum beat, the second dance was more restrained, though without doubt it also was a warriors' dance. Quiet in step and color, men and women danced together, first forming one long line, then facing each other. There were also very small boys dancing and hopping with the mastery of lifelong experience. All the dancers had eagle feathers fastened to the crowns of their heads. The men were nude except for the ceremonial buckskin kilt. Every other man had painted his face and the upper part of his body black—and a queer glittering black it was that he had under his eyes—and on his kilt he had the image of the horned serpent; while the alternate men had splotches of white all over their bodies and a white

68

serpent coiling up their left arms. The men carried a rattle in the right hand and a bow in the left. The women held a bunch of arrows in both hands.

The rhythm of the dance was restrained, yet its quality was more insistent and stirring than that of the preceding dance. It seemed as if the warriors had changed the church into the kiva, stamping the ground as if calling the spirits from *shipap* beneath, summoning the beings who had met death and therefore gained the power to bless life. The songs sung by the chorus, far in the rear of the church, sounded like incantations in a minor key and resembled the muffled whirr of wings and sometimes the distant rumble of thunder. But ever and again a sudden shriek flared up, swooping down upon the dancers, who then quickened the rhythm of their steps and the intensity of their gestures. The leader of the ceremony stood apart from the choir and, like a conductor, by performing a superb dance on the spot, seemed to direct and inspire the dancers from an inexhaustible reservoir of spiritual strength.

While the men and women were facing each other, the men rhythmically moved their bows toward their partners, and the women responded by passing their arrows up and down. This pantomime left no doubt about the ultimate purpose of the dance. The power that was produced by way of step and song and, above all, by way of a very subtle imitative magic, was supposed to mingle with the power that radiated from the miraculous presence of María and José, up there on the altar. With the progress of the dance, a sense of utmost confidence seemed to spread: in due time the seed would germinate, the corn would grow, the harvest be abundant.

And then, when the dance had come to an end, it was indeed a moving sight to watch the warriors pass by and move up to the altar and kiss María ceremonially—with their eagle feathers whipping, *Avanyu* coiling on kilt and bare arm, deer-hoofs rattling, bells chiming, and bear-claw necklaces suggesting great strength and aggressive power.

While the dancers were filing out and vanishing into the drizzling night, the birds redoubled their twittering, and old men went about distributing gifts to the children—apples, nuts, and such good things. Before long, however, another group of dancers ranged into the church, escorted to position by the leader and the drum beater. This group instantly diffused an atmosphere of utmost solemnity, though their costumes at first seemed incongruous. The young men— no women danced—wore crowns built up out of various feathers, paper flowers and many-colored ribbons. At the napes of their necks dangled fluffy bunches of turkey feathers. Their black, wide-sleeved shirts— remindful of Russian blouses—were crisscrossed with long flowing ribbons, gathered here and there and held together by Navajo clips. All of them wore high brown Navajo moccasins trimmed with silver buttons. In the left hand they carried bow and arrows adorned with blue and red ribbons, in the right hand a rattle. There was no separate chorus; the dancers themselves sang. And they danced with a sense of deep seriousness, subdued somewhat and as if overshadowed by a presence, invisible but weighty and even threatening. Though the beater of the drum—a beautiful, large drum it was, covered with a white skin—occupied a more important position ceremonially than the drum beaters of the two preceding dances, it was neither he nor even the young men who represented the central part of the dance. It was the leader who obviously had the "power." He was the man who had "talked with the gods," and who therefore knew and had wisdom, though he was young. He was the man without flaw or blemish, perfect in spirit and body. It was he who imbued the dance with its almost trenchant quality of austerity. Skipping along the line of young men, he held every single dancer in his spiritual grip. He was authoritative but not despotic; imperative but not without benevolence.

His body was painted white. An animal pelt was wagging at the rear of his kilt, and he held another pelt in his left hand. Around his head he wore a beaded band in which was stuck a very long, slender feather tipped with eagle down. This feather whipped resolutely, responding to every move, to every step and gesture, accentuating the stringent nature of every single turn of his body. Choreographically, his performance was unique and of a rare, mature beauty, perhaps for the simple reason that there was not a gesture that did not serve a spiritual purpose, not a step but was patterned according to an age-old group experience and had, therefore, become an instinct. He had an inimitable way of changing abruptly from a brisk walking step into a vigorous dance step. Sometimes he paused for a moment, overlooking the file of dancers, quivering with alertness and yet perfectly self-controlled, only to snap back into action without warning, stamping the ground, making queer angular motions with his arms, angular and yet graceful, steeling the youths with strength, infusing them with his own power. And this seemed to be the ultimate purpose of this dance: accumulation of power, sheer, blind power. Whether it was intended to be used for good or for evil, who could tell? Perhaps, too, this dance had something to do with the Navajo, once the fiercest enemy of the sedentary Puebleños. Either it commemorated a victory over the one-time enemy, or it symbolized preparation for an attack. It is hard to tell.

However, María and José were still sleeping together on the altar, and the spiritual inflexibility of the leader and the somber seriousness of the youths seemed to melt into an attitude of mellow devotion when they all filed up to the sanctuario, one by one, to pay homage before the couple and bend their knees and kiss María. I, too, walked up once more to have a look at María and José and the animals. And when I turned around, a San Felipan stood behind me, with a friendly smile on his face, and he gave me an apple. At any time it is pleasant to be presented with an apple; but at this time and at this place it seemed to me to be a particularly good and happy omen. And thus came to a close the Christmas Eve at San Felipe.

SECTION ONE:

From the Northern Woodlands, the Basin Area, and the Great Plains

SONG

SUNG OVER A DYING PERSON
(CHIPPEWA)

You are a spirit,
I am making you a spirit,
In the place where I sit
I am making you a spirit.

Frances Densmore, *Chippewa Music I,* p. 95. This is a
song which would be sung when a member of the *Mide-
wiwin* was dying—when death was expected at any moment.

DREAM SONG

(CHIPPEWA)

In the Sky
I am walking,
A Bird
I accompany.

From *ibid.* II. This is a song which came to the mind
of an Indian in a dream. "Many Indian songs," says Miss
Densmore in her admirable work on Chippewa music, "are
intended to exert a strong mental influence, and dream
songs are supposed to have this power in greater degree
than any others. The supernatural is very real to the In-
dian. He puts himself in communication with it by fasting
or by physical suffering. While his body is thus subordinated
to the mind a song occurs to him. In after years he believes
that by singing this song he can recall the condition under
which it came to him—a condition of direct communication
with the supernatural." *Ibid.* I, p. 118.

LOVE SONG

(CHIPPEWA)

Oh
I am thinking
Oh
I am thinking
I have found my lover
Oh
I think it is so!

From *ibid.* II, p. 300. The Chippewa lover intersperses his songs with the music of the flute, while other songs are usually accompanied by either the drum or the rattle. The Chippewa expresses every phase of his life, every mood, in music and in song. But not the words are considered the essential part of this particular song, it is the melody, the peculiar rhythm, that conveys the meaning of the song more directly than any words could do.

A WOMAN'S SONG

(CHIPPEWA)

You are walking around
Trying to remember
What you promised,
But you can't remember.

From Frederick R. Burton, *American Primitive Music*,
p. 277. Chippewa songs are concise and compact. They are
seldom complete in themselves, for usually they are only
the mnemonic summaries of a long-trailing story. Frequently
they are preluded by the singer with an explanation. The
above song, however, does not need any explanation.

LOVE SONG

(CHIPPEWA)

A loon I thought it was
But it was
My love's
Splashing oar.

From Frances Densmore, *op. cit.* I, p. 89. This lovely poem, composed of but a few words, though full of overtones and hints of things unsaid, bears such a strange resemblance to those exquisite little poems of classic Japanese literature that I cannot refrain from calling the reader's attention to this fact. In order to understand part of the American Indian's poetry one must be well trained in swiftly reacting upon the faintest suggestions, intimations, and symbols. He very often gives only the mere outline of a fleeting mood or of the lasting impression of an experience —opening in himself or in the listener a train of thoughts and emotions: just what makes Japanese poetry—on a different level, to be sure—stand out so vividly from the more eloquent ways of the western poets.

PRAYER TO THE SUN
(Blackfoot)

Okōhe! okōhe! natosi! iyo!
Sun, take pity on me; take pity on me.
Old age, old age,
We are praying to your old age,
For that I have chosen.
Your children, morningstar, seven stars, the bunched
    stars, these and all stars,
We can call upon them for help.
I have called upon all of them.
Take pity on me;
Take pity on me that I may lead a good life.
My children, now I have led them to old age.
That which is above, now I choose, take pity on me.
Iyo!
Old age, let me lead my children to it.
Let me get a stock of many horses . . .
Take pity on me that I get the full pay for all my work.
Iyo!
Take pity on me; take pity on me; take heed.

From Clark Wissler, *Ceremonial Bundles of the Blackfoot
Indians*, p. 252. Says Wissler: "It is scarcely too much to
say that the Blackfoot are given to inordinate prayer. They
will pray for permission to speak of sacred things, to tell
religious narratives, in fact to do any unusual serious thing."
And he continues: "A distinguished leader of ceremonies
said that in prayers, as well as in all work with rituals, the
officiator should keep his attention fixed upon the desired
end. 'Keep thinking of it all the time,' he advised." And
then success would be certain.

THE BUFFALO ROCK
(Northern Blackfoot)

The first people, those are the ones that found the buffalo rock. Nearly starved were all the people. A man said to his wife, "Get some wood and build a fire." She said, "I am not strong enough; I am nearly starved." "Go on," said he, "there is no firewood here." Then she arose, saying, "I shall go after firewood." She came to a place where there was wood, and, standing beside it, picked it up slowly. Then she heard singing and looked around. At last she saw it. On the cut-bank's side she sat down. The thing doing the singing was the buffalo rock. The earth was sliding down: that is how she came to see it. While it was singing, the rock said:

"Take me,
I am powerful."

On buffalo hair it was sitting for a bed. It stretched out its arms. In order that food might be obtained is the reason she saw it. She took it up, wrapped it in the hair and put it inside her dress. Now she knew some food would be obtained. She went back to the camp. She went to her husband's lodge. She went inside. She said to her elder sister, "Tell our husband that I shall make medicine." So the elder one said to him, "My younger sister is about to make medicine." He said, "I have faith. Let her make medicine that we may have food." Then he called out, inviting the camp. All came to the lodge—men, women and children—all came inside. "There is going to be medicine," he said. "Get some tallow," said he, "just a little." Then everyone looked for it. A long time they had to hunt before finding any.

Then the woman rubbed the fat on the rock. It began to sing when she did it. It sang to the woman:

"Take me,
I am powerful."

The people all saw it. The woman passed it to them, and they kissed it. "You shall have food," she said. Then she began to sing and then to dance. All joined in the dancing. They made a noise like buffalo. The woman sang, "A hundred I shall lead over the drive." She said, "When you sing, do not say more than a hundred." Now a man said when he sang, "Over a hundred shall I lead over the drive." The woman said, "We have made a mistake now. So many will go over that the enclosure will burst; they will jump out of it. There will be a solitary bull wandering through the camp tonight. It will be a mangy bull. No one shall kill him. . . . If that bull comes tonight, we shall all be saved. If this rock falls on its face, then you will all be happy. There will be plenty of food." All went out. They were happy, because they were to receive food. The woman slept where the smudge was made. That rock made her powerful.

He came through the camp, the one she said was coming—the mangy bull. They all knew him. They all said, "Ah— a! don't kill him. Rub his back with firewood." In the morning all were happy because the mangy bull came at night. They did not kill him, the one that was said to come at night. When the woman looked out, that rock fell over on its face. Then she told them to be happy, because they would have something to eat. Looking up, the people saw many buffalo close to the camp. Then the swift young men went out and led the buffalo, many of them. They worked them into the lines. They frightened them to make them run swiftly. Then all ran over into the enclosure. Now the people ran there. Inside were the buffalo. So many were there that the enclosure was broken. Over a hundred were there. That is why they broke down the fence. Not many of them were killed. All the buffalo were bulls. That is why they broke down the fence.

The woman's husband took all the ribs and back-fat, saying, "With these shall a feast be made. Again my wife will make medicine." The people were some-what happy, the number of animals killed was small. "For a little while we are saved. We have a little meat," said the man.

The next night it was called out again that the woman was to make medicine. This time she gave orders that only the women were to dance, so that cows might come to the drive. So the women danced. The men tried not to make another mistake. In the morn-ing they looked from the hill again. They were made glad by the rock falling again on its face. Again the young men went out. Now all in the enclosure were cows. They were all killed with arrows. None of them got out. The people were happy now. They had plenty of meat. Everyone now believed in the power of the rock. The woman who found the rock was respected by her husband.

Clark Wissler, *Mythology of the Blackfoot Indians,* pp. 87-9. Taken as a text by Dr. R. Lowie.

THE ORIGIN OF DEATH
(Coeur D'Alêne)

Once a woman had twin children who fainted away. Possibly they only slept. Their mother left them in the morning; and when she returned in the evening, they were still lying there. She noticed their tracks around the house: therefore she thought they must come to life and play during her absence. One day she stole on them unseen and found them arguing with each other inside the lodge. One said, "It is much better to be dead." And the other said, "It is better to be alive." When they saw her, they stopped talking, and since then people die from time to time. There are always some being born and some dying at the same time, always some living ones and some dead ones. Had she remained hidden and allowed them to finish their argument, one would have prevailed over the other, and there would have been either no life or no death.

James Teit in Franz Boas, ed., *Folk-Tales of Salishan and Sahaptin Tribes*, p. 125.

SMOHALLA SPEAKS
(NEZ PERCÉ)

My young men shall never work. Men who work cannot dream, and wisdom comes in dreams.

You ask me to plow the ground. Shall I take a knife and tear my mother's breast? Then when I die she will not take me to her bosom to rest.

You ask me to dig for stone. Shall I dig under her skin for bones? Then when I die I cannot enter her body to be born again.

You ask me to cut grass and make hay and sell it, and be rich like white men. But how dare I cut off my mother's hair?

It is a bad law, and my people cannot obey it. I want my people to stay with me here. All the dead men will come to life again. We must wait here in the house of our fathers and be ready to meet them in the body of our mother.

See Herbert J. Spinden: *The Nez Percé Indians,* p. 261, and B. Alexander, *Mythology of North America,* p. 150. The Nez Percé Indians belong to the Sahaptin stock and culturally and geographically to the Great Basin area. Thus their culture was a composite of elements derived partly from the Plains, partly from the Pacific coast. Agriculture was absent before the coming of the white man. Various kinds of roots formed the staple of their diet. Their religious concepts were of marked simplicity. No cosmogonic myths; little ceremonialism. The dream was the chief means of communication with the spiritual world. It was perhaps due to the paucity of their religious traditions that the Nez Percés first took eagerly to the teachings of the Christian missionaries. It is a much-quoted story how they even delegated a group of chiefs to Saint Louis asking impatiently for ministers and the new powerful Book of the white man. However, it was a Nez Percé—Smohalla—who founded the Dreamer Religion, falling back on the native concepts, especially those of the benign Earthmother and the dream as the only vehicle of supernatural power. He opposed vigorously the inroads of the white man and his civilization, especially all attempts to introduce agriculture in his domain. He influenced later developments of the Ghost Dance elsewhere; this ceremony itself, however, never struck root among the Nez Percés. See Spinden, *op. cit.,* pp. 258-61.

THE SURRENDER SPEECH OF
CHIEF JOSEPH
(NEZ PERCÉ)

I am tired of fighting. Our chiefs are killed. Looking Glass is dead. Toohulhulsote is dead. The old men are all dead. It is the young men who say no and yes. He who led the young men is dead. It is cold and we have no blankets. The little children are freezing to death. My people, some of them, have run away to the hills and have no blankets, no food. No one knows where they are—perhaps they are freezing to death. I want to have time to look for my children and see how many of them I can find. Maybe I shall find them among the dead. Hear me, my chiefs, I am tired. My heart is sad and sick. From where the sun now stands I will fight no more forever.

From Spinden, *op. cit.,* p. 243. Oratory, says Dr. Spinden, was a highly developed art among the Nez Percés, "for on this depended much of the power and prestige of the chiefs. The rule of the council was unanimity, and this would be effected only by calm reasoning where facts were to be considered, and by impassioned appeal when the decision depended on sentiment. There was considerable use of gesticulation and a great display of dignity. Statements were concise and concrete."

TWO MORNING SPEECHES
(Nez Percé)

1. The Herald Rides around the Camp

I wonder if everyone is up! It is morning. We are alive, so thanks be! Rise up! Look about! Go see the horses, lest the wolf have killed one! Thanks be that the children are alive! And you, older men!—and you, older women! also that your friends are perhaps alive in other camps. But elsewhere there are probably those who are ill this morning, and therefore the children are sad, and therefore their friends are sad.

2. Speech before a War Dance

People, lay everything aside, for now we are going to have a dance. Get out your finest clothes and put them on, and make ready for the dance. People, we shall see the garments of our dead men of long ago; so everyone must come, because another time we may not be living. . . .

From Herbert J. Spinden in Franz Boas, ed., *Folk-Tales of Salishan and Sahaptin Tribes*, p. 201. These are two examples of the more or less stereotyped pronouncements of the herald who rides around the village or the camp and gives the orders of the day.

COTTONTAIL BOY AND SNOWSHOE RABBIT

(NEZ PERCÉ)

There were Cottontail Boy and his friend Snowshoe Rabbit. It was cold, very cold. Cottontail Boy lived by the river in its warmth, and there he would say, "I wonder what my friend Snowshoe Rabbit could be doing there far yonder where the gray coldness looms."

But the Snowshoe Rabbit was saying the same, "I wonder what my friend Cottontail Boy could be doing there where the blue haze of warmth looms."

One day they met.

"So, my friend, we meet. Is it that you are in good health?"

"Eh! I should be asked when you are the one! I used to think about you, 'What things could my friend be doing there where the blue haze of warmth looms?'"

"Is that it? Well, I am just living very, very comfortably," Cottontail Boy said to him. "Here I have such a good, very warm lodge under a beautiful overhanging cliff. There I kick up a hackberry bush by the roots and I bring this home to burn. This now burns so well, and then I take root food over which I pour water and the water is absorbed instantly. I recline comfortably there now and eat very heartily, so heartily. But I thought of you often and I would say to myself, 'What can my friend be doing there where the gray coldness looms?'"

"Oh, I, too, live just comfortably from day to day," Snowshoe Rabbit told him. "I have a very comfortable living place. There is a big growth on a pine tree, and my home is there at the root. Here I may just kick apart fallen chunks of wood to burn. Oh, how this now burns coals and ashes! Then I take fatty dried meat and toast it somewhat to a red crispness. There I lean back and eat so heartily. . . ."

"Yes, it seems that both of us are living very well."

Then they said to each other, "Farewell, we will meet again sometime."

From Archie Phinney, *Nez Percé Texts*, p. 3. The delightful stories of this volume were recorded on the Fort Lapwai Reservation and obtained from a sixty-year-old woman, Wayílatpu, the mother of the recorder. Humor, says Phinney in the Introduction, is undoubtedly the most vivid element in these Nez Percé tales, and it permeates both the commonplace and the tragic. Myth and folktale of this Sahaptin tribe is, however, in the state of slow disintegration, due, as the collector of these stories says, to "a morbid reservation consciousness." The young Indian tries to forget the past, and the sense of humor, so characteristic of this folklore, gives way to the vulgar which is considered to be funny.

WARRIOR SONG
(CROW)

Eternal are the heavens and the earth;
Old people are poorly off.
Do not be afraid.

From Robert H. Lowie, *The Religion of the Crow In-dians*, p. 417. The Warrior Wants-to-die, whose possession the above song was, addressed a group of youths who were about to enter the warpath, like this: "When a woman gives birth, it takes her a long time and she does not know whether she will live or not. You have it easy, the camp is right here. Mount your horses and go, there is nothing to hold you back. When you get there, you will either be killed or will kill an enemy. Let me know how your heart is." And after he made up his mind to accompany them, he added: "Let us all mount our horses. When I am old, I shall die. I will die at any time; I want to find out how it is. It is like going up over a divide."

THE SEVEN STARS
(Assiniboine)

There were seven youths on this world. One of them was red-haired. They did not know whether they had any parents. They were having a hard time of it. "What shall we turn into?" they asked one another. One said, "Let us change into the earth." The one named the Wise-one (Ksábe) said, "No, verily the earth is mortal, it gets caved in." Then another one said, "Let us become rocks." "No, they are destructible, they all break asunder." A third one said, "We must change into big trees, into very big ones." "No, they are perishable, when there is a storm they are blown down." Again one of them said, "Let us change into water." "No, it is destructible, it dries up completely." The fifth said, "Let us change into the night." "No, the night is fleeting, soon the light appears again." The sixth boy said, "Let us be the day." "No, it is fleeting, when the sun disappears, it is dark once more." The Wise-one said, "The blue sky above is never dead, it is always in existence. Shining things live there. Such we shall change into. In that region let us dwell."

Well, so they do. The smallest of them took them up, hoisting them by means of his spider web. He set three on one side and three on the other, seating himself in the middle. When the last one had gotten up, he tore the web in the middle, threw it down, and gave it to the spider.

From Robert H. Lowie, *The Assiniboine*, p. 177.

PRAYER

(ASSINIBOINE)

Spirits of our dead relatives, I make this feast for you to call you all around me. I smoke this tobacco which has been inclosed with your hair; be near us and hear.

My friends are around me, and you are called to the feast. Call on all the spirits of our dead friends to aid in giving us what we ask.

Make the buffalo come near and the clouds and wind fair to approach them, that we may always have meat in camp to feed us and you. Help us in every way; let our children live. Let us live. Call on all these spirits and ask them to assist you in helping us.

If we hunt, be with us. If we go to war, be with us. Enable us to revenge some of your deaths upon our enemies. They have killed you; they have brought our hearts low. Bring their hearts low also. Let us blacken our faces. Keep us from harm, rest quiet, we will not cease to cry for and remember you. You are remembered in this feast, eat some of it [here small bits are scattered around]. This to you, my father. This for you, my grandfather, my uncle, my brother. The relatives of all present eat, rest in quiet, do not let disease trouble us.

We eat for you, we cry for you, we cut ourselves for you.

From Edwin T. Denig, *Indian Tribes of the Upper Missouri*, p. 284. The Assiniboine are a typical Plains tribe,

93

living in the region northwest of the great bend of the Missouri. Predatory warfare, buffalo hunting and, in later days, horse raiding, were those occupations by which a man, if he carried them on with success, acquired status within his group. However, a man participated in any of these activities only if a favorable dream or vision and the unmistakably demonstrated good will of his tutelaries, or the spirits of the dead, promised success.

PRAYER OF A WARRIOR
(ASSINIBOINE)

O Wakonda, you see me a poor man.
Have pity on me.
I go to war to revenge the death of my brother.
Have pity upon me.
I smoke this tobacco taken from my medicine sack,
where it has been enveloped with the remains of my
dead brother [a lock of his hair]. I smoke it to my
tutelary, to you; aid me in revenge.
On my path preserve me from mad wolves.
Let no enemies surprise me.
I have sacrificed, I have smoked, my heart is low,
have pity upon me. Give me the bows and arrows of
my enemies. Give me their guns. Give me their horses.
Give me their bodies. Let me have my face blackened
on my return. Let good weather come that I can see.
Good dreams give that I can judge where they are. I
have suffered. I wish to live. I wish to be revenged. I
am poor. I want horses. I will sacrifice. I will smoke.
I will remember. Have pity on me.

From Edwin T. Denig, *Indian Tribes of the Upper Mis-
souri*, pp. 483-4. Denig wrote his report about 1854.

MYTH OF CREATION
(Osage)

Way beyond, a part of the Osage lived in the sky. They desired to know their origin, the source from which they came into existence. They went to the sun. He told them that they were his children. Then they wandered still farther and came to the moon. She told them that she gave birth to them, and that the sun was their father. She told them that they must leave their present abode and go down to the earth and dwell there. They came to the earth, but found it covered with water. They could not return to the place they had left, so they wept, but no answer came to them from anywhere. They floated about in the air, seeking in every direction for help from some god; but they found none. The animals were with them, and of all these the elk was the finest and most stately, and inspired all the creatures with confidence; so they appealed to the elk for help. He dropped into the water and began to sink. Then he called to the winds, and the winds came from all quarters and blew until the waters went upward as in a mist.

At first rocks only were exposed, and the people traveled on the rocky places that produced no plants, and there was nothing to eat. Then the waters began to go down until the soft earth was exposed. When this happened, the elk in his joy rolled over and over on the soft earth, and all his loose hairs clung to the soil. The hairs grew, and from them sprang beans, corns, potatoes, and wild turnips, and then all the grasses and trees.

From Alice Fletcher and Francis LaFléche, *The Omaha Tribe*, p. 63.

FROM THE RITE OF VIGIL

Wi'gi-e
of the Symbolic Painting
(OSAGE)

With what shall they adorn their bodies, as they tread
the path of life? it has been said, in this house.

The crimson color of the God of Day who sitteth in
the heavens,
They shall make to be their sacred color as they go
forth upon life's journey.

Verily, the God who reddens the heavens as he
approaches,
They shall make to be their sacred color, as they go
forth on life's journey.

When they adorn their bodies with the crimson hue
shed by that God of Day,
Then shall the little ones make themselves to be free
From all causes of death, as they go forth on life's
journey.

What shall the people use for a symbolic plume?
They said to one another, it has been said, in this
house.
Verily, the God who always comes out at the beginning
of day,

Has at his right side
A beam of light that stands upright like a plume.
That beam of light shall the people make to be their
sacred plume.

98

What shall they place as a pendant upon his breast?
They said to one another.
The shell of the mussel who sitteth upon the earth,
They shall place as a pendant upon his breast.
It is as the God of Day who sitteth in the heavens,
Close to his breast they shall verily press this god,
As a pendant upon his breast they shall place this god.

Then shall the little ones become free from all causes
Of death, as they go forth upon life's journey.

From Francis LaFlésche, *The Osage Tribe: The Rite of Vigil*, p. 74. This Rite of Vigil was performed in times of distress in order to bring the people in close touch with the Supernatural Power. This rite can be observed as well collectively as individually. At any time during the summer —when nature "is fully awake and active"—the man stricken with grief by the loss of some beloved person may take upon himself this rite in seeking pity from the Mysterious Power. The Osage Indian, whose life is replete with sun-symbolism, experiences the sun as the visible manifestation of the Highest Power; above all, he glorifies the regularity of the movements of the "God of Day."

THE SONG OF THE MAIZE
(Osage)

Amid the earth, renewed in verdure,
Amid rising smoke, my grandfather's footprints
I see, as from place to place I wander,
The rising smoke I see as I wander.
Amid all forms visible, the rising smoke
I see, as I move from place to place.

Amid all forms visible, the little hills in rows
I see, as I move from place to place.

Amid all forms visible, the spreading blades
I see as I move from place to place.

Amid all forms visible, the light day
I see as I move from place to place.

From Francis LaFlésche, *The Osage Tribe,* pp. 634-5.
It is the spirits of the dead who are speaking in this song. It
is they who see first the joyful signs of the awakening of
the earth from the long spell of winter. In the smoke that
rises in the early morning from the fields where the women
are planting the precious maize seeds, they sense, amid the
secret processes of growing and ripening, the presence of a
divine power: the mysterious footprints in the soft earth,
what else do they intimate than the path of the Mysterious
Ones who crossed the fields to urge onward the growing
corn to maturity?

THE WEAVER'S LAMENTATION

(Shrine Ritual)

(OSAGE)

[The cry of longing and desolation uttered by the weaver in the following song is for her relatives who had gone on to the spirit land and who had been close companions in the joys and griefs of life.]

You have left me to linger in hopeless longing,
Your presence had ever made me feel no want,
You have left me to travel in sorrow.
Left me to travel in sorrow; Ah! the pain,
Left me to travel in sorrow; Ah! the pain, the pain,
    the pain.

You have left me to linger in hopeless longing,
In your presence there was no sorrow,
You have gone and sorrow I shall feel, as I travel,
    Ah! the pain, the pain.

You have gone and sorrow I shall feel as I travel,
You have left me in hopeless longing.
In your presence there was no sorrow,
You have gone and sorrow I shall feel as I travel;
    Ah! the pain, the pain, the pain.

Content with your presence, I wanted nothing more,
You have left me to travel in sorrow; Ah! the pain,
    the pain, the pain!

From *ibid.*, p. 697.

A WARRIOR'S SONGS FROM THE
MOURNING RITE
(OSAGE)

1.

Behold, I go forth to move around the earth,
Behold, I go forth to move around the earth,
I go forth as the puma that is great in courage.
To move onward I go forth,
I go forth as the puma that is great in courage.
Behold, I go forth to move around the earth.

Wi'gi-e

O Hon'ga and Wa-zha'zhe,
Verily, I am a person who has made a god to be his
    body,
The god of night,
I have made to be my body,
Therefore I am difficult to be overcome by death.
O, Hon'ga and Wa-zha'zhe,
If you also make that god to be your body,
You also shall be free from all causes of death.

2.

Behold, I go forth to move around the earth,
Behold, I go forth to move around the earth,
I go forth as the great black bear that is great in courage.
To move onward I go forth,

I go forth as the great black bear that is great in courage.
Behold, I go forth to move around the earth.

From Francis LaFlésche, *The War Ceremony of the Osage Indians*, pp. 123-4. The Mourning rite had its origin in the vision of an individual mourner: while wandering about out in the solitude of the uninhabited prairie, wailing and fasting, the relative for whom he was mourning appeared, asking him to slay an enemy whose spirit could accompany him to the land of the setting sun, for the journey to this country was long and lonely and fearsome. Ever since, when a death had occurred among the Osage, a war party was sent out to retrieve a scalp of an enemy whose soul was supposed to accompany the spirit on his last journey. A *wi'gi-e* is a recitative, relating part of a mythical story.

A WARRIOR'S SONG OF DEFIANCE

From the War Ceremony

(OSAGE)

You speak to me of dangers that I may fear,
But I have willed to go, my friends.
Waxada-in's crying stirs my wrath,
I go forth to strike, even Wa-kon-da, should
    He oppose me.
You speak to me of dangers that I may fear.
But I have willed to go, my friends.

From *ibid.,* p. 31. The *Wa-shábe A-thin,* or War Cere-
mony, was performed when the aggressions of the enemy
became intolerable, and at the same time there was a feel-
ing of indifference àmong the warriors toward the taking of
retaliatory measures (p. 4). By way of elaborate ceremonies
the Leader aimed at exciting enthusiasm among the young
warriors.

THE HEAVENS ARE SPEAKING
(PAWNEE)

1.

I stood there, I stood there,
The clouds are speaking.
I say, "You are the ruling power,
I do not understand, I only know what I am told,
You are the ruling power, you are now speaking,
This power is yours, O heavens."

2.

It is there that our hearts are set,
In the expanse of the heavens.

From Frances Densmore, *Pawnee Music,* pp. 88, 90. Before recording the first song Frances Densmore's informant spoke the following sentences, accompanying the words with slow drum beats: "The song which I am about to sing belonged to Man Chief. When he became chief he used to go out into the storm. . . . He heard Tirawa speak through the clouds. He knew the heavens were the ruling power, and he prayed for his people."

THE CORN SPIRIT

(Skidi Pawnee)

A man was roaming over the prairie. He came to a place where people had camped and there he heard a woman crying. The man went to the place where the crying came from, but there was no one there, and he did not know what to think. When he went home he lay down, and in the night he had a dream. He dreamed that he saw a woman. The woman spoke to him and said:

"I stay where the crying came from, and I was glad that you hunted me and tried to find me. I am going to help you to find me, and also let you see me. As soon as the sun goes down and it becomes a little dark, I want you to go to the place where you heard the crying. I will be there, and there you shall see me and I will tell you some things that you do not know."

When the man awoke he thought of the woman he was to see that evening, and so he watched and looked over the country until the sun went down. He watched the women passing through the village, and as soon as the sun disappeared and it became a little dark he went to the place where he had heard the crying. As soon as he arrived at this place, instead of hearing the crying he saw a woman. The woman spoke to the man and said: "Look, look at me, for I am the one who was crying at this place." The man looked at the woman and he saw that she was a fine-looking woman. She said again: "Young man, when the people passed over this place while hunting buffalo they dropped me. I have been crying ever since." . . . Then the woman said: "Look upon the ground where my feet rest." The man looked and there he saw a kernel of corn. This kernel of corn was speckled. "Now," said the woman, "pick up this kernel of corn and keep me always with you. My spirit is of Mother-Evening-Star, who gives us the milk that is in the corn. The people eat of us and have life. The women give the same milk from their breast. Keep me in your quiver and my spirit will always be with you."

The man took the kernel up and the woman disappeared. The man went home and kept the kernel close to him all the time. . . . He put the kernel of corn into a bundle and the bundle became a sacred bundle. . . . The young man became a great warrior. Once he said: "In the tribe is a nice-looking girl whom I like." The Corn-Woman spoke to him in a dream and said: "I do not want you to marry for two seasons. When you have received my spirit and you understand me, then you shall marry. You must tell your mother to place me in a large hill of earth. When a stalk grows from the hill and you find corn upon the stalk do not eat it, but lay it away. Then the next spring tell your mother to plant some more corn and the next fall there will be a good crop and you will see how the corn has multiplied." The young man did as he was told. As the spring came the mother placed the kernel in a big hill of earth. And a stalk grew out of this hill with many kernels upon it. These she laid away until the next spring. Then she planted much more corn.

About that time the young man married. The young man and his wife had many children, and their children had children. When Corn-Woman disappeared she told the man to tell his people, when they were ready to plant corn, to pray first to Mother-Corn and then to Mother-Earth. "When you have placed the corn in the earth then stand to the west and pray to Mother-Evening-Star to send rain upon the earth so that the corn will grow. Pray also to Mother-Moon, who helps give life to people, and she will listen to what people say. Never drop a kernel upon the ground, for Mother-Corn will curse you and your life will be shortened."

Corn-Woman also told the young man that when the cornfields were high, all the people were to take their children into the fields and to pass their hands over the stalks and then over the children. Thus the children would grow, and bad diseases would go away from them. Corn-Woman also said: "When the tassels are out, then watch. There will be singing in the fields. Know that that singing comes from the sacred ear of the corn. Take it from the stalk, and take it to the old man, who will place it in the sacred bundle so that people will know that Mother-Corn did sing to her people." The Pawnee worship Mother-Corn because she represents Mother-Evening-Star.

From George A. Dorsey, *The Pawnee Mythology*, pp. 58-61. A few lines have been omitted.

WAR SONG
(Pawnee)

Let us see, is this real,
Let us see, is this real,
This life I am living?
Ye Gods, who dwell everywhere,
Let us see, is this real,
This life I am living?

From Daniel G. Brinton, *Essays of an Americanist,* p.
292. This is, says Brinton, a war song with a curious meta-
physical turn. It is sung when a warrior goes out all alone
on the warpath from which it is likely he will never return.

THE POOR BOY AND THE MUD PONIES
(Pawnee)

A long time ago there were no horses. Dogs were the only animals that helped the people carry the burdens. In those times there was a very poor boy in the village. He went from one tepee to another trying to get something to eat. Sometimes he was chased out, but at other times he was taken in and fed.

Once in a great while he would go into the lodge of the chief, and when the chief would see him he would feel sorry for him and sometimes he would give him moccasins; at other times he would give him leggings. Some people would speak against the boy and try to keep the chief from giving him any presents, but the chief would say: "Tirawa knows that this boy is living. As he is growing up he will watch over him and the boy may some day rule over us." But the people laughed at the chief for saying that.

The boy had a dream about ponies. He thought that two ponies were dropped down from the heavens and that they were for him. He so plainly saw the ponies in his dream that he knew their shape, and how their tails and manes looked. Often when the people broke camp and traveled along he would stay behind and would take mud and make ponies. Then he would place the ponies in his robe and follow the people. Before he would arrive at the village he would place the two mud ponies outside of the village. Early in the morning he would go to where his mud ponies were. Then he would take the mud ponies down to the creek and pretend that they were drinking. He did this for many months, until the people had returned to their permanent village. Then he took the mud ponies and carried them a long way from the village and stood them by a pond. He would go away and stay for a while and then return and make believe the ponies needed water. Then he would take them to where there was good grass and place them there.

One night the boy had a dream. He thought that Tirawa had opened the sky and dropped two ponies for him. Then he thought in his dream that he heard Tirawa singing and he remembered well the song, for when he awoke he went out from the lodge and went up on a high hill, and there he sang the song. The people heard him singing and they wondered what that song meant. While the boy was singing, a mysterious voice said: "This song was given to you by Tirawa. Tirawa has given you a dance. You shall become a chief. Go this night to where your mud ponies are and there you will find two live ponies." The boy ran. When he arrived there he saw two ponies. The two ponies came to the boy and he caught both of them. The people went out to see the ponies and almost worshipped them, for they were the first they had ever seen.

From G. A. Dorsey, *The Pawnee Mythology*, p. 123.

SPIRIT LAND

Told by Cheyenne-Chief

(PAWNEE)

There was a village, and among the people was a man who had a beautiful wife. He thought much of her and spent his time in hunting game, so that they might have plenty to eat.

After a time they had a son, who grew up. When he was about twelve years old his mother died. Then the man took good care of the boy, for he was his only son. The boy became sick and died.

The man did not know what to do, whether to kill himself or to wander over the country. He decided to wander over the country. He mourned four days at the grave of his son; now he was to roam over the country. He went many days, and after a while he came to some timbered country. He went through it. He had his quiver filled with arrows and a bow. While in this timber he heard people talk in his language, and he stopped. . . . One came to him and said: "What a wonderful tree! All of you come! I have found a wonderful tree. It looks like a man." The man stood still, and the others came and said: "Truly this is a wonderful tree. Look, it has eyes, nose, and hair! Look, here is a quiver and bow." At this saying the man shrieked, and said: "I thought you were all dead! Here you are wandering over the country." As soon as he spoke they ran away. He could hear some of them say, "He has caught me!" Another would say, "He has caught my foot," when the creature was caught by briers and grapevines. They ran a long way, then they stopped; and they began to tell how narrowly they had escaped from the man.

While they were talking, the man came upon them again, and away they went. The man followed them up. This time they disappeared on the side of a hill, and, as it was now late in the day, the man made up his mind to follow and to try and stand with them. He thought, as he was wandering, "Why not remain with these people?" He got to the place where they had disappeared, and under a thick grapevine found an entrance large enough for a man to crawl in; there, far within, was a cave. He knew the leader. He had carried the sacred bundle and had led the war party; but he now saw them and knew they were lost; that they had been attacked by the enemy, and that they had been scalped. He sat there looking at them. They were talking about him. The man did not go entirely inside, for he himself was afraid. While they were talking, someone shrieked, "There he is!" and they would pile themselves one on top of another. . . .

The leader, who was sitting under the bundle, said: "Boys, keep quiet! This man is of our people. Get up and make a fire, and we will hear what he has to say." Fire was made, and each took his place where he belonged in the circle. And then the leader asked him what brought him there.

"Nava," said the man, "I lost my wife. We had a son and he died, too. I was left all alone. I have mourned for him a long time, longing for death, so that I might join my wife and son. I wandered from home until I came here. I am here, and I am glad I can now make my home with you, my brothers; for I do not care to be with my people any more."

The leader spoke and said: "It is good, but we cannot let you live with us. We are dead. What you see are spirits. We should have gone to the Spirit Land but for this bundle which you see. It belongs to our people, and Tirawa released our spirits, so that we could wander back and return the bundle. Brother, I am glad you came to us. We will teach you the ceremony of this bundle; then take it home, and let our people know that the bundle is again found."

The man sat a long time, for he knew that to accept what this man said was to become a power among his people and be a leader. But at last he spoke and said: "My people, I am poor in heart. I cannot accept what my brother has offered, for I am never to return to my people. If I cannot see my son I am ready to die." Here he stood up and continued: "My brothers, take pity on me; take me with you to Spirit Land that I can see my boy. I cannot take the bundle to my people, for I am not happy." He passed his hands over the leader's head and on down the arms. "Take pity on me," he said once more.

The leader sat with downcast head. Then he stood up, took down the bundle, took out sweet grass and put it in the fire, then opened the bundle. He looked at all the things in the bundle; he took them outside, so that the gods who gave them might look at them. Then he said: "My brothers, I must help this man to remain here. I will go to the gods in the west, who will receive this man's words. I pity him. I think the gods will pity him. I go."

He disappeared. The others watched and watched.

At last they heard the wind descend. The leader had come back. He went to the bundle, took out native tobacco and burnt it, offering it to the gods. Then he spoke: "My son, the gods in the west have received your words. All the gods sent their words to Tirawa, and Tirawa has given his consent for the people in Spirit Land to come and see the living. They are to camp with them four days and four nights, without speaking one to another. You are to be allowed to be near your son and to speak with him, but not to touch him. . . . Those who wish to remain with their relatives as well as those who wish to go to Spirit Land will be permitted to do so. Now, my son, go. Get your people. Let them come and make their camp in the neighborhood."

So the man left that same night. He noticed that he was very swift. Why, he could not understand. Finally he reached the village. A crier was called and told to go through the camp and let the people know that they were wanted at a certain place; that they were to meet their dead friends.

The next day they broke camp and went south. For a long time they traveled, until finally they came to a timbered country. Here they pitched their camp. The man went to the camp of the spirits. He was told that the dead people were also on the way, and that the next morning they would arrive. The man went to the camp, and notified the crier to go quietly and tell the people to be ready to see their friends. Some mocked and others believed. . . .

The next day people began to make preparations to meet their dead friends. Medicine ointment was put upon their heads, faces, and hands. Some time in the afternoon they saw a great dust which reached the heavens. People began to get frightened; others rejoiced, for they were again to see their dead friends. People rejoiced with song. Then the spirits began to pass through. As they passed, the people saw their dead friends, but they did not dare to touch or speak to them. As they kept up the marching, the man's son came. He caught his son. Now he was told . . . not to speak [touch?] to him. . . . He did not do this, for as soon as he caught his son he spoke to him and hugged him, and in his heart he said: "I will not let you go!"

As soon as this was done the spirits went off. The other spirits also disappeared. The man went away broken-hearted. The people returned home, and the man never came back. The people said: "He is with the scalped men." But afterwards he was seen, and had over him a horse robe. He was wild, did not seem to care to be with his people. So he was forgotten; for had he not caught his son, then the spirits and the people were to have lived once more together, and death was to have been unknown.

From George A. Dorsey, *Traditions of the Skidi Pawnee,* pp. 74-8. A few lines have been omitted.

COYOTE AND THE ORIGIN OF DEATH

(Caddo)

In the beginning of this world there was no such thing as death. Everyone continued to live until there were so many people that there was no room for any more on the earth. The chiefs held a council to determine what to do. One man arose and said that he thought it would be a good plan to have the people die and be gone for a little while, and then to return. As soon as he sat down Coyote jumped up and said that he thought that people ought to die forever, for this little world was not large enough to hold all of the people, and if the people who died came back to life, there would not be food enough for all. All of the other men objected, saying that they did not want their friends and relatives to die and be gone forever, for then people would grieve and worry and there would not be any happiness in the world. All except Coyote decided to have the people die and be gone for a little while, and then to come back to life again.

The medicine men built a large grass house facing the east, and when they had completed it they called the men of the tribe together and told them that they had decided to have the people who died come to the medicine house and there be restored to life. The chief medicine man said they would sing a song that would call the spirit of the dead to the grass house, and when the spirit came they would . . . restore it to life again. All of the people were glad, for they were anxious for the dead to be restored to life and come again and live with them.

After a time—when the first man had died—the medicine men assembled in the grass house and sang. In about ten days a whirlwind blew from the west and circled about the grass house. Coyote saw it. And as the whirlwind was about to enter the house, he closed the door. The spirit in the whirlwind, finding the door closed, whirled on by. Death forever was then introduced, and people from that time on grieved about the dead and were unhappy.

Now whenever anyone meets a whirlwind or hears the wind whistle he says: "There is someone wandering about." Ever since Coyote closed the door, the spirits of the dead have wandered over the earth, trying to find some place to go, until at last they find the road to Spirit Land.

Coyote jumped up and ran away and never came back, for when he saw what he had done he was afraid. Ever after that he ran from one place to another, always looking back first over one shoulder and then over the other, to see if anyone was pursuing him, and ever since then he has been starving, for no one will give him anything to eat.

From George A. Dorsey, *The Traditions of the Caddo*, pp. 15-16.
The Coyote plays a conspicuous part in the stories of creation and transformation of the North American Indian. The Coyote is the prairie wolf, a small, greedy and cowardly animal. He is mostly represented as the sly and deceitful trickster who is always about to thwart the plans of the benevolent but by no means all-powerful creator god. At

times he merely imitates in a ridiculous way the works of the Maker or the culture hero. And yet, with all this, he not seldom is shown as the culture hero himself, as the powerful magician who not only destroys but also brings about order in this chaotic world. With all his mean selfishness he displays at times an astonishing amount of cleverness and sound judgment. Coyote tales are at home in the western part of the northern continent. His eastern counterpart is the Great Hare.

THE REQUEST FOR SUPERNATURAL HELP

(TETON SIOUX)

[Siyáká' speaks:]

All classes of people know that when human power fails they must look to a higher power for the fulfillment of their desires. There are many ways in which the request for help from this higher power can be made. This depends on the person. Some like to be quiet, and others want to do everything in public. Some like to go alone, away from the crowd, to meditate upon many things. In order to secure a fulfillment of his desire a man must qualify himself to make his request. Lack of preparation would mean failure to secure a response to his petition. Therefore when a man makes up his mind to ask a favor of Wakan'tanka he makes due preparation. It is not fitting that a man should suddenly go out and make a request of Wakan'tanka. When a man shuts his eyes, he sees a great deal. He then enters his own mind, and things become clear to him, but objects passing before his eyes would distract him. . . . [So] he resolves to seek seclusion on the top of a butte or other high place. No man can succeed in life alone, and he cannot get the help he wants from men; therefore he seeks help through some bird or animal which Wakan'tanka sends for his assistance.

From Frances Densmore, *Teton Sioux Music*, p. 184.

TWO DREAM SONGS OF SIYÁKÁ'
(TETON SIOUX)

1.

At night may I roam
Against the winds may I roam
At night may I roam
When the owl is hooting
May I roam.

At dawn may I roam
Against the winds may I roam
At dawn may I roam
When the crow is calling
May I roam.

2.

Where the wind is blowing
The wind is roaring
I stand.

Westward the wind is blowing
The wind is roaring—
I stand.

From *ibid.*, p. 186. Dream songs are the most precious spiritual possession of the individual, received by the vision-seeking youth, after much suffering and loneliness, in a dream. The obligation of a dream, says Miss Densmore, was as binding as the necessity of fulfilling a vow. That the wished-for dream would correspond to the character of the man was recognized by the Sioux. The nature of the dream allied the man to others who had similar dreams. "If the dreams were connected with the sacred stones, or with herbs concerned in the treatment of the sick, it was considered obligatory that the man avail himself of the supernatural help vouchsafed to him in the dream, and arrange his life in accordance with it." p. 157.

OPENING PRAYER OF THE SUN DANCE
(Teton Sioux)

Grandfather!
A voice I am going to send,
Hear me!
All over the universe
A voice I am going to send,
Hear me,
Grandfather!
I will live!
I have said it.

PRAYER SPOKEN DURING THE
SUN DANCE
(Teton Sioux)

Wakan'tanka
When I pray to him
Hears me.
Whatever is good he
Grants me.

From *ibid.,* pp. 131, 140.

TWO SONGS OF ENCOURAGEMENT
(TETON SIOUX)

1. War Song

Soldiers,
You fled.
Even the eagle dies.

2. Council Song

Friends,
With all manners of difficulties
I have been pursued.
These I fear not.
Still
Alive I am.

From *ibid.*, pp. 394, 449.

SONG OF A MAN WHO RECEIVED A VISION
(TETON SIOUX)

Friends, behold!
Sacred I have been made.
Friends, behold!
In a sacred manner
I have been influenced
At the gathering of the clouds.
Sacred I have been made,
Friends, behold!
Sacred I have been made.

From *ibid.*, p. 165.

SONG OF FAILURE
(Teton Sioux)

A wolf
I considered myself,
But the owls are hooting
And the night
I fear.

From *ibid.*, p. 339.

LAST SONG OF SITTING BULL
(TETON SIOUX)

A warrior
I have been.
Now
It is all over.
A hard time
I have.

From *ibid.*, p. 459. Sitting Bull sang this, his last song, after he had surrendered to the United States authorities, some time after the Custer massacre.

OHIYESA REMEMBERS THE PAST
(Sioux)

As a child I understood how to give; I have forgotten this grace since I became civilized. I lived the natural life, whereas I now live the artificial. Any pretty pebble was valuable to me then; every growing tree an object of reverence. Now I worship with the white man before a painted landscape whose value is estimated in dollars! Thus the Indian is reconstructed, as the natural rocks are ground to powder and made into artificial blocks which may be built into the walls of modern society.

The first American mingled with his pride a singular humility. Spiritual arrogance was foreign to his nature and teaching. He never claimed that the power of articulate speech was proof of superiority over the dumb creation; on the other hand, it is to him a perilous gift. He believes profoundly in silence—the sign of a perfect equilibrium. Silence is the absolute poise or balance of body, mind, and spirit. The man who preserves his selfhood is ever calm and unshaken by the storms of existence—not a leaf, as it were, astir on the tree; not a ripple upon the surface of the shining pool—his, in the mind of the unlettered sage, is the ideal attitude and conduct of life.

If you ask him: "What is silence?" he will answer: "It is the Great Mystery!" "The holy silence is His voice!" If you ask: "What are the fruits of silence?" he will say: "They are self-control, true courage or endurance, patience, dignity, and reverence. Silence is the cornerstone of character."

"Guard your tongue in youth," said the old ⟨
Wabashaw, "and in age you may mature a tho
that will be of service to your people!"

From Charles Alexander Eastman, *The Soul of the In-dian.* Eastman (Ohiyesa) was born near Redwood Falls, Minnesota, in 1858. His father was a full-blooded Sioux, his mother the daughter of an army officer, granddaughter of a famous Sioux chief. As a boy he lived still the free nomadic life of the Sioux; later, however, he took up the ways of the white man, went to college, graduated 1887 at Dartmouth College, N. H., whereupon he took a medical course at Boston University.

129

A WOMAN JOINS HER LOVER IN DEATH
(DAKOTA)

There was a big hill, a butte, where years ago a war party was held at bay till all the members died; and none escaped, they say. And it was there that the people stopped, on a journey, and stood looking for a suitable place to make camp, when this, which I am about to relate, took place.

At the foot of that butte there was already a camp; and this group came to it and stopped, when a woman, her shawl pulled up over her head, started to sing:

> "There was a man I loved, alas!
> Can it be that I shall see him again,
> My own?"

With such words she stood on the hilltop, singing. As the tribe fixed their attention singly on her, she started taking dancing steps backwards, and allowed herself to fall headlong over the cliff, landing, all bruised and broken, among the rocks below. She was dead. So they took up her body and carried it to her tepee, but her husband, evidently jealous, did not so much as weep a tear; but said, instead: "No, do not bring her here. Take her back, she has announced that she loved him; so let her rot with him!" So they could not enter her tepee with her body. Instead they took it back and left it where she fell. And they came away. So, there with him, who from all appearances was her lover, she mingled her bones, and they together in time became as dust, just as she desired in her song.

Then a crier went around announcing a removal of

the camp. It was according to the magistrate's decision. They said: "There is no other way; we cannot stay here. We must move from this spot where such a foul deed has taken place." So, in spite of the fact that camp had just been made, they all packed in haste and moved away that same evening.

From Ella Deloria, *Dakota Texts,* p. 261. Ella Deloria is a Teton, trained by Franz Boas to take down the stories of her own people.

Suicide is not uncommon among several Indian tribes. Frustration in love is the main motive. Incest tabus, making marriage between two parallel cousins impossible, led not infrequently to joint suicide, even among the more primitive tribes such as the Shoshoneans of the Great Basin. However, suicide was not always considered a disgrace to the group, but was rather treated like any other form of death.

A SONG OF THE HEYOKA CEREMONY
(DAKOTA)

This I burn as an offering.
Behold it!
A sacred praise I am making.
A sacred praise I am making.
My nation, behold it in kindness!
The day of the sun has been my strength.
The path of the moon shall be my robe.
A sacred praise I am making.
A sacred praise I am making.

From John G. Neihardt, *Black Elk Speaks, the Life Story of an Oglala Sioux.* The outstanding feature of the Heyoka ceremony is that it is made up by funny actions. This is what the medicine man Black Elk tells about this ceremony: "When a vision comes from the thunder beings of the west, it comes with terror like a thunderstorm; but when the storm of vision has passed, the world is greener and happier; for wherever the truth of vision comes upon the world, it is like a rain. The world, you see, is happier after the terror of the storm. But in the Heyoko ceremony, everything is backwards, and it is planned that the people shall feel jolly and happy first, so that it may be easier for the power to come to them. You have noticed that the truth comes into the world with two faces. One is sad with suffering, and the other laughs; but it is the same face, laughing or weeping. When people are already in despair, maybe the laughing face is better for them. . . ." p. 192.

WARRIOR SONG OF THE HETHUSHKA SOCIETY

(OMAHA)

I shall vanish and be no more,
But the land over which I now roam
Shall remain
And change not.

From Fletcher and LaFlésche, *The Omaha Tribe.* The object in establishing the Hethúshka society was "to stimulate an heroic spirit among the people and to keep alive the memory of historic and valorous acts. . . . It was a rule of the society that when a member performed a brave deed the society was the authority to decide whether the name of the doer and the record of his deed should be preserved in song." The Omaha informant explained the above song in the following manner: "The natural fear of death that is in every individual sometimes so overpowers a man that in the time of danger he may lose self-control and abandon to their fate those whom he is in duty bound to protect. To drive away the fear of death . . . the members were persistently taught that man's life is transitory, and being so it is useless to harbor the fear of death, for death must come sooner or later to everybody; man and all living creatures come into existence, pass on and are gone, while the mountains and the rivers remain ever the same—these alone of all visible things abide unchanged." p. 475.

WARRIOR SONG
(Omaha)

No one has found a way to avoid death,
To pass around it;
Those old men who have met it,
Who have reached the place where death stands
    waiting,
Have not pointed out a way to circumvent it.
Death is difficult to face.

From *ibid.*, p. 431.

TRIBAL PRAYER

(Omaha)

Wa-kon'da,
here needy he stands,
and I am he.

From Alice Fletcher, *Indian Story and Song*, p. 26. The
tribal prayer, says Alice Fletcher, was called in the Omaha
tongue *Wa-kon'da gikon: Wa-kon'da*, the power which can
bring to pass; *gikon*, to weep from conscious insufficiency,
or the longing for something that could bring happiness or
prosperity.

FAREWELL, MY NATION! FAREWELL, BLACK HAWK!

From *The Autobiography of Black Hawk,* dictated by himself to Antoine LeClair, 1833.

Soon after our return home, news reached us that a war was going to take place between the British and the Americans.

Runners continued to arrive from different tribes, all confirming the reports of the expected war. The British agent, Colonel Dixon, was holding talks with, and making presents to, the different tribes. I had not made up my mind whether to join the British or remain neutral. I had not discovered yet one good trait in the character of the Americans who had come to the country. They made fair promises but never fulfilled them, while the British made but few, and we could always rely implicitly on their word.

One of our people having killed a Frenchman at Prairie du Chien, the British took him prisoner and said they would shoot him next day. His family were encamped a short distance below the mouth of the Wisconsin. He begged for permission to go and see them that night as he was to die the next day. They permitted him to go after he had promised them to return by sunrise the next morning.

He visited his family, which consisted of his wife and six children. I cannot describe their meeting and parting so as to be understood by the whites, as it appears that their feelings are acted upon by certain rules laid down by their preachers, while ours are governed by the monitor within us. He bade his loved ones the last sad farewell and hurried across the prairie to the fort and arrived in time. The soldiers were ready and immediately marched out and shot him down.

[Interrupting the straight course of his account he says in melancholy:]

Why did the Great Spirit ever send the whites to this island to drive us from our homes and introduce among us poisonous liquors, disease, and death? They should have remained in the land the Great Spirit allotted to them. But I will proceed with my story. My memory, however, is not very good since my late visit to the white people. I have still a buzzing noise in my ears. . . . I may give some parts of my story out of place, but will make my best endeavor to be correct.

[Some chiefs were called upon to go to Washington to see the Great Father, who wanted them in case of war to remain neutral, promising them to let the traders sell to them in the fall goods on credit, that they might hunt and repay with furs in the spring, as the British had arranged it up to then. Everything depended for the Sac upon this institution. But—the trader refused bluntly to sell on credit.]

The war chief said the trader could not furnish us on credit, and that he had received no instructions from our Great Father at Washington. We left the fort dissatisfied and went to camp. What was now to be done we knew not. . . . Few of us slept that night. All was gloom and discontent.

[As a result of this treatment they joined the British.]

Our lodges were soon taken down, and we all started for Rock Island. Here ended all hopes of our remaining at peace, having been forced into war by being deceived. . . .

We continued our march, joining the British below Detroit, soon after which we had a battle. The Americans fought well and drove us back with considerable loss. I was greatly surprised at this, as I had been told that the Americans would not fight. . . .

On my arrival at the village I was met by the chiefs and braves and conducted to the lodge which was prepared for me. After eating, I gave a full account of all that I had seen and done. I explained to my people the manner in which the British and Americans fought. Instead of stealing upon each other and taking every advantage to kill the enemy and save their own people as we do, which with us is considered good policy in a war chief, they march out in open daylight and fight regardless of the number of warriors they may lose. After the battle is over they retire to feast and drink wine as if nothing had happened. After which they make a statement in writing of what they have done, each party claiming the victory and neither giving an account of half the number that have been killed on their own side.

[The British lose constantly. After a long time of consideration and many councils Black Hawk decides to make a treaty of peace with the "chief at St. Louis."]

The great chief at St. Louis having sent word for us to come down and confirm the treaty, we did not hesitate but started immediately that we might smoke the peace pipe with him. On our arrival we met the great chiefs in council. They explained to us the words of our Great Father in Washington, accusing us of heinous crimes and many misdemeanors, particularly in not coming down when first invited. We knew very well that our Great Father had deceived us and thereby forced us to join the British, and could not believe that he had put this speech into the mouths of those chiefs to deliver to us. I was not a civil chief and consequently made no reply, but our civil chiefs told the commissioners: "What you say is a lie. Our Great Father sent us no such speech, he knew that the situation in which we had been placed was caused by him." The white chiefs appeared very angry at this reply and said, "We will break off the treaty and make war against you, as you have grossly insulted us."

Our chiefs had no intention of insulting them and told them so, saying, "We merely wish to explain that you have told us a lie, without any desire to make you angry, in the same manner that you whites do when you do not believe what is told you." The council then proceeded and the pipe of peace was smoked.

Here for the first time I touched the goose quill to sign the treaty, not knowing, however, that by the act I consented to give away my village. Had that been explained to me I should have opposed it and never would have signed their treaty, as my recent conduct will clearly prove. What do we know of the manners, the laws, and the customs of the white people? They might buy our bodies for dissection, and we would touch the goose quill to confirm it and not know what we were doing. This was the case with me and my people in touching the goose quill the first time.

139

We can only judge of what is proper and right by our standard of what is right and wrong, which differs widely from the whites', if I have been correctly informed. The whites may do wrong all their lives and then if they are sorry for it when about to die, all is well, but with us it is different. We must continue to do good throughout our lives. If we have corn and meat, and know of a family that have none, we divide with them. If we have more blankets than we absolutely need, and others have not enough, we must give to those who are in want.

[As Black Hawk could not yield to the demand of the "white chiefs" and leave his village and his graveyard, a war ensued, the so-called Black Hawk War, lasting from 1831-2. Chief Keokuk, his great antagonist, who was willing to negotiate with the whites and persuaded part of the tribe to abandon the village, caused thus a rift among the Sac.]

I looked upon Keokuk as a coward and no brave. . . . What right had these people [the whites] to our village and our fields, which the Great Spirit had given us to live upon? My reason teaches me that land cannot be sold. The Great Spirit gave it to his children to live upon and cultivate as far as necessary for their subsistence, and so long as they occupy and cultivate it they have the right to the soil, but if they voluntarily leave it, then any other people have a right to settle on it. Nothing can be sold but such things as can be carried away.

[It was at Fort Crawford that Black Hawk, in the despair of defeat, said: "Farewell, my nation! Farewell, Black Hawk!"]

The massacre which terminated the war lasted about

two hours. Our loss in killed was about sixty, besides a number that was drowned. . . .

I was now given up by the agent to the commanding officer at Fort Crawford, the White Beaver [General Atkinson] having gone down the river.

On our way down I surveyed the country that had cost us so much trouble, anxiety, and blood, and that now caused me to be a prisoner of war. I reflected upon the ingratitude of the whites when I saw their fine houses, rich harvests, and everything desirable around them; and recollected that all this land had been ours, for which I and my people had never received a dollar, and that the whites were not satisfied until they took our village and our graveyards from us and removed us across the Mississippi.

On our arrival at Jefferson Barracks we met the great war chief, White Beaver, who had commanded the American army against my little band. I felt the humiliation of my situation; a little while before I had been leader of my braves, now I was a prisoner of war. He received us kindly and treated us well.

We were now confined to the barracks and forced to wear the ball and chain. This was extremely mortifying and altogether useless. Was the White Beaver afraid I would break out of his barracks and run away? Or was he ordered to inflict this punishment upon me? If I had taken him prisoner on the field of battle I would not have wounded his feelings so much by such treatment, knowing that a brave war chief would prefer death to dishonor. But I do not blame the White Beaver for the course he pursued, as it is the custom among white soldiers, and I suppose was a part of his duty.

BLACK HAWK'S DEDICATION TO GENERAL ATKINSON

Sir— The changes of fortune and vicissitudes of war made you my conqueror. When my last resources were exhausted, my warriors, worn down with long and toilsome marches, yielded, and I became your prisoner. The story of my life is told in the following pages: it is intimately connected, and in some measure identified with a part of the history of your own: I have, therefore, dedicated it to you.

The changes of many summers have brought old age upon me, and I cannot expect to survive many moons. Before I set out on my journey to the land of my fathers, I have determined to give my motives and reasons for my former hostilities to the whites, and to vindicate my character from misrepresentations. The kindness I received from you whilst a prisoner of war assures me that you will vouch for the facts contained in my narrative, so far as they came under your observation.

I am now an obscure member of a nation that formerly honored and respected my opinions. The pathway to glory is rough, and many gloomy hours obscure it. May the Great Spirit shed light on yours, and that you may never experience the humiliation that the power of the American government has reduced me to, is the wish of him who, in his native forests, was once as proud as you.

10th Moon 1833.   BLACK HAWK

Preceding *The Autobiography of Black Hawk.*

A SEQUENCE OF SONGS OF THE GHOST DANCE RELIGION

1.

My children,
When at first I liked the whites,
I gave them fruits,
I gave them fruits.

2.

Father have pity on me,
I am crying for thirst,
All is gone,
I have nothing to eat.

3.

The father will descend,
The earth will tremble,
Everybody will arise,
Stretch out your hands.

4.

The Crow—*Ehe'eye!*
I saw him when he flew down,
To the earth, to the earth.
He has renewed our life,
He has taken pity on us.

143

5.

I circle around
The boundaries of the earth,
Wearing the long wing feathers,
As I fly.

6.

I'yehé! my children—
My children,
We have rendered them desolate.
The whites are crazy—Ahe'yuhe'yu!

7.

We shall live again,
We shall live again.

Selected from James Mooney, *The Ghost Dance Religion.*
These seven songs, composed by Plains Indians amid the
blissful state of a trance induced by dancing, may stand for
the various threads that made up the web of this religious
ceremony, a last creative outburst of a race that was doomed
to vanish.

The songs in the above sequence bring into relief a few
of the elements of this composite religious movement—that
is, in its later manifestations: sincere welcome of the white
man and his astonishing new ways of life followed by bitter
disillusionment and the consciousness of being forsaken
even by their own gods. But out of deceit, rottenness, and
wanton destruction arises the Messianic vision of a new
god who will mercifully renew their life, and, after having
annihilated the "crazy" whites—a trait particularly devel-

oped by the Smohalla cult—call back the glories of the past, if only upon another plane of existence.

However, it is not Mooney's much-quoted work on the Ghost Dance that provides us with the historical background and opens up the psychic milieu of this religious movement that swept across the Plains in 1890. It is Leslie Spier's *The Prophet Dance of the Northwest* (1935) that, by means of elaborate documentation both from historic sources and ethnographic materials, challenges the hitherto accepted supposition that these nativistic movements were nothing but "cults of despair" sprung up merely as a reaction against the demoralizing influences of the whites and the contact with Christianity. Spier proves that, on the contrary, these religious revivals were deeply rooted in an aboriginal pattern. The Ghost Dance of 1890 was not a wholly new development, but had its historical antecedent in the Prophet Dance of the Northwest, the doctrine of which—"belief in the impending destruction and renewal of the world, when the dead would return," was native. Even the later Smohalla cult was essentially, not Christian. It was ready to assimilate elements of the Christian belief only on account of a certain doctrinal similarity. Spier's study offers to the student of cultural processes material of great psychological interest. On the one side, it cautions the overeager student as to the nature of cultural similarities: similar patterns may very well have developed independently. And, on the other side, new traits are usually acculturized more or less successfully only if aboriginal patterns and attitudes bear a certain resemblance to the features to be assimilated. This latter fact should have considerable bearing on the activities of "cultural engineers."

THE MAN WHO WAS IN SEARCH
OF THE MANITOUS
(Fox)

This is about one man a long time before the white men came here. As I relate this today, it is not really I who is responsible: it is narrated as I heard the narrators. And if they made mistakes in what they said I shall indeed make mistakes in what I say when narrating this today. But I shall tell the story very carefully as the old men told me. I shall surely narrate it exactly as I heard it. That is how this story will be. Would that I were older, for then I might tell a very interesting tale. . . .

A long time ago when this earth was young, whoever existed as mortal and fasted earnestly finally was richly blessed, it is said, by the manitous.

But nothing happened to him (that young man). He did not even have a name, as he was very poor. He looked again and again at the Spirit of Fire, it seems, so it is said. Finally, as he was gazing at the Spirit of Fire, it blazed, so it is said. "Well," he said, "this one is greatly endowed with mystic power," he thought, it is said. "Tomorrow I shall go and wail," he thought, "for I know all too little how my life is. I do not even know how my life will be in the future," he thought, it is said.

So, early the next morning, he started to take down his tobacco and burned it for the Spirit of the Fire. "Now, my grandfather, today I give you this tobacco to smoke as I wail for my life," he said to him. As he went out he shrieked blindly as he wandered far off in the wilderness. He went about wailing. And when he saw anything that appeared mysterious, he took his tobacco and cast it on it. "My grandfathers! Manitous! Because I am indeed wretched is why I go about wailing," he said, it is said. . . .

Finally he walked back to where he came from and ate.

And the next morning he went far off, blindly with open hands, that he might know where the manitous dwelt. He simply thought anything was a manitou and scattered his tobacco. Well, in exactly ten days he came back to eat. That verily is what I narrate. He did not know anything. Therefore he again departed. And he came back. He had been going about wailing the third time. And again he merely ate and departed, it is said. That indeed is what happened to him. So, it is said, he was addressed by a manitou. It was a wolf. It was a black one, it is said. "Now today, my grandchild, I bless you," he said. He was blessed by a manitou, a black wolf. "But myself I am not able to bless you, so that my blessing will be valid," the wolf said to him. "But let us go yonder," he was told. And he was taken to the east, it is said. "Now this day I bring my grandchild. I took pity upon him as he wailed bitterly because he did not know how his life was. He thought his life was very wretched. That is why I took pity upon him," this wolf said to this manitou who dwells in the east. "Surely I also take compassion upon him in the same way," they were told by the manitou. "You must indeed in addition take him yonder. For as we are now merely two who bless him, it is not enough," said this manitou. So they went out again, departed

147

and went to where a manitou dwelt in the south, it is said. That verily is what is related. [And] he was blessed in every kind of way, even so that he himself might bless the people.

From Truman Michelson, *Fox Miscellany*, pp. 102-3. The beginning of a ritual origin myth, told in a rather rambling style, but typical both in content and form of narration.

THE MAN WHO REPROACHED THE
MANITOUS

(Fox)

Now this is an old story of what the people a long while ago, a very long while ago, did, some time before the white man came here on this island [earth].

Now it seems there was a man, a young man, who married. He was a fine fellow. After he married, soon he had a child. Well, soon when it had grown large, their little son began to be ill. He became sicker, and sure enough their little son died. Soon after their son died his wife likewise began to be ill. It was for a short time, and then she also died.

After his son and wife died, then it seems he began fasting in the winter, wailing all the while. "Surely the manitou could not have made us," he cried out. He went around weeping and putting down tobacco, giving everything, even water, a smoke. "Well, I hand this tobacco to you as I do not know what my future life will continue to be," he said to water, rocks, and every little thing that looked strange to him. Suddenly he made burnt offerings [of tobacco] to trees, wailing all the while. Soon he went around wailing at dusk. This is how he sang when he went around wailing:

"Cry, cry for myself—
Cry, cry for myself."

That, it seems, is the song he used.

"Where, pray, are ye, manitous," he said. And he said to the manitous, "Why do you make mortals as they die?" He quarreled with them without reason. "Have pity upon me," he said to them. As often as it was winter for four years that man, it seems, fasted far off. He who found the little buffalo was the one first to be blessed. Finally, it seems that later on he was soon addressed by one being. "Well, try to cease wailing; I shall bless you," he was told. "Verily, I in turn shall live with you as long as this earth remains on earth, such is the extent of the blessing I bestow upon you. . . . For I know how badly you felt when you lost sight of your son whom you loved."

From Truman Michelson, *On the Fox Indians*, p. 507. Sam Peters, a Fox Indian, put the text down in his native language, while T. Michelson translated it literally.

A SPEECH TO THE DEAD
(Fox)

Now this day you have ceased to see daylight.
Think only of what is good.
Do not think of anything uselessly.
You must think all the time of what is good.
You will go and live with our nephew.
And do not think evil towards these your relatives.
When you start to leave them this day you must not
    think backwards of them with regret.
And do not think of looking back at them.
And do not feel badly because you have lost sight of
    this daylight.
This does not happen today to you alone, so that you
    thus be alone when you die.
Bless the people so that they may not be sick.
This is what you will do.
You must merely bless them so that they may live as
    mortals here.
You must always think kindly.
Today is the last time I shall speak to you.
Now I shall cease speaking to you, my relative.

From *ibid.*, p. 417.

LAMENTATION
(Fox)

It is he, it is he,
The person with the spirit of an owl;
It is he, it is he,
The person with the spirit of an owl;
It is he, it is he.

All the manitous are weeping,
Because I go around weeping,
Because I go around weeping,
All the manitous are weeping.

The sky will weep,
The sky,
At the end of the earth;
The sky will weep.

From Truman Michelson, *The Owl Sacred Pack of the Fox Indians,* p. 29. With the Fox, mourning for the individual dead is deep and passionate, but their attitude toward death in general is stoic: the Fox is expected to face death without fear and cowardice, for no one can escape it. Said Owl in times way back: ". . . we shall not live here forever. We shall die. In fact, we shall all die. No one of us who exist as mortals here, shall exist as a mortal forever. As many of us as blink have death, all of us who call each other mortals. If anyone thinks, 'No, not I; I shall always exist as a mortal,' he surely dies. He surely comes to death. For he, the manitou, has fixed that which will happen to each one of us." p. 55. The Owl is sacred to the Fox.

SPEECH OF THE OWL
(Fox)

My grandchildren, I bless you. There is nothing evil
in the way I have thought of you. I have thought of
you indeed in a good way. So long as your life shall
endure, so long shall I make it go for you. And from
time to time you will continue to gladden the people
by what you do: such is the blessing I shall continue
to bestow upon you. But, my grandchildren, *do not
expect anything in return from your fellow-people
whom you have pleased.* That is the only thing I tell
you.... Do not throw me out of your thoughts. Verily
I too have put my thoughts in here [in the sacred bun-
dle] when I blessed you. When I think of going yonder
I go thither. *I arrive at where I am going.* Even if
there were a river flowing by, I would come there,
nothing would go wrong with me; even if there were
a cliff where I was going I should go there. I should
not be hindered at all. . . . That is one way I bless
you. If a river is deep and wide, you will easily wade
across.

And again, if anyone is wounded, you will heal him.
You will not fail to heal him, but only if he prays to
you; if he does not pray to you, you will not heal
him. . . . Even if anyone's bone is broken, you will
heal it together for him. . . . But you will live quietly.
You will have plenty of time to share it with others.
But there is this: you will instruct those who will take
care of the sacred pack in the future, that each may
take extremely good care of it; and you will accord-

ingly tell them that they continue to hold gens festivals with solemnity; and you will accordingly tell them that they always think seriously of it. . . .

The one that will truly continue to believe you is the one that will continue to be blessed by the sacred pack here. And the one who shall not believe you will not continue to be blessed in the future. *The one that continues to think of it is the one that will be thought of.* He will not become sick. Moreover, if your foes fight with you, he is the one who will not be shot. *And some will think you funny.* Such a one will truly die . . .

And all the manitous will hear the flute when you blow it. As many times as you blow it, he will hear it, though its sound does not go very far. But even the one who is above will hear it.

You will truly please me if you do not cease thinking of what I tell you. . . . I myself will be close by there to listen to you. And do not think little of it. When you tell the young people, even if they poke fun at you, you shall tell them quietly. Do not think of speaking harshly. You will think, 'Of course quietness is the only way.' . . .

And I shall give you this pipe. You shall smoke it twice during the entire summer. This is why you all should smoke, that you be not afflicted with disease. That is why you should smoke. Verily, after gens festivals the people will be in good health. No one shall go away continuing to be in bad health. If any goes about in bad health, if he smokes, he will straightway have good health.

Now what I tell you will come to pass. So you must zealously endeavor to carefully think of it. I am not speaking to you for fun. Exactly what I say to you shall come to pass. Nor shall I bless you here for a little while when I think of you. Until this earth ceases to be an earth, is as far as it will take care of you, if you always think seriously of it, and if you keep on holding gens festivals.

From *ibid.*, pp. 41, 43, 45. A "sacred bundle" is anything that has "power." The ritual that is always associated with a bundle has the purpose to keep alive the rapport between the supernatural source of the sacred pack and the owner; it also serves to transfer the power from the original owner to another person. See Wissler, *Ceremonial Bundles of the Blackfoot Indians*, p. 272.

THE STORY OF MY ANCESTOR WESHGISHEGA

(WINNEBAGO)

When Weshgishega was growing up his father coaxed him to fast. He told him that when Earthmaker had created the various spirits, all the good ones he had created were placed in charge of something. The gift of bestowing upon man life and victory in war he gave to some; to others, the gift of hunting powers. Whatever powers the Indians needed in order to live, these he placed in the hands of various spirits. These blessings Weshgishega's father told Weshgishega to attempt to obtain from the spirits.

Thus Weshgishega fasted and tried to obtain something from the spirits. But as he fasted he kept thinking to himself, "Long ago Earthmaker created all the different spirits and he put every one of them in control of something, so people say. He himself must therefore be much more powerful than all the others. As holy as these spirits are, so assuredly Earthmaker must be mightier, holier." So he thought. He tried to be blessed by Earthmaker. He thought to himself, "What kind of being is he?" As he fasted Weshgishega thought to himself, "Not even any of the spirits whom Earthmaker created has really known Earthmaker as he actually is; not one of the spirits has he even blessed. I wonder, however, whether Earthmaker would bless me? This is what I am thinking of." So he put himself into a most pitiful condition and uttered his cry to the spirits. He could not stop. "From Earthmaker do I wish to obtain knowledge. If he does not bless me during my fasting I shall assuredly die." So, to the utmost of his power did he fast. He wished to be blessed only by Earthmaker.

At first he fasted four days; then six; then eight; then ten, and finally twelve days. After that he broke his fast. Yet it was quite clear that he had obtained no knowledge, quite clear that he had not been blessed. So he gave up his fasting and when he reached the age of early manhood he married.

He took his wife, and the two of them moved to an out-of-the-way place. There they lived, he and his wife.

Here again he commenced to fast, his wife with him. He wished to be blessed by Earthmaker. This time he felt that most assuredly would he die if Earthmaker did not appear before him in his fasting. "Never has it been told that such a thing could happen, that Earthmaker would bless anyone. Yet I shall continue even if I have to die."

After a while a child was born to him. It was a boy. He addressed his wife and asked her advice, saying that they ought to sacrifice their child to Earthmaker. She consented. To Earthmaker therefore they prepared to sacrifice their child. They constructed a platform and placed their child upon it. Then both of them wept bitterly. In the nighttime when the man slept, Earthmaker took pity on him and appeared to him. The man looked at him. He thought, "This, most certainly, is Earthmaker." He wore a soldier's uniform and carried a high cocked hat on his head. He had a very pleasing appearance. Weshgishega looked at him and wondered whether this really was Earthmaker. The figure took one step, then another, and finally disappeared, uttering a cry. It was not Earthmaker; it was a pigeon. The bad spirits were fooling Weshgishega.

Now even more than before did his heart ache, even more than before was his heart wound up in the desire to be blessed by Earthmaker. Now again he fasted and again apparently Earthmaker appeared to him. "Human being, I bless you. Long have you made your cry for a blessing. I am Earthmaker." When Weshgishega looked at him, he saw that he was pleasing in appearance. He looked very handsome and his dress was nice to look upon. He wondered whether this really was Earthmaker. As he looked at the figure it became smaller and smaller and when finally he looked, he noticed that it was a bird.

Then his heart ached even more than before. Bitterly did he cry. Now, for the third time, Earthmaker blessed him saying, "Human being, you have tried to be blessed by Earthmaker and you have caused yourself great suffering. I am Earthmaker and I bless you. You will never be in want of anything; you will be able to understand the language of your neighbors; you will have a long life; indeed, with everything do I bless you." But, from the very first, this figure did not inspire Weshgishega with confidence and he thought to himself, "Somebody must be fooling me." And so it was; it was a bird.

Then most assuredly did he think that he wished to die, for he felt that all the bad birds in the world were trying to make fun of him.

Earthmaker, above where he sits, knew of all this. He heard the man's voice and he said, "O Weshgishega, you are crying. I shall come to the earth for

158

you. Your father has told me all." Then when Wesh-gishega looked, he saw a ray of light extending very distinctly from the sky down to the earth. To the camp it extended. "Weshgishega, you said that you wanted to see me. That, however, cannot be. But I am the ray of light. You have seen me."

Not with any war powers did Earthmaker bless him; only with life.

From Paul Radin, *Crashing Thunder*, pp. 20-3.

A PRAYER
(Winnebago)

Hearken, O Earthmaker, our father, I am about to offer tobacco to you. My ancestor concentrated his mind upon you, and that with which you blessed him I now ask of you directly. I ask for the small amount of life you granted him, and for four times the blessings you bestowed upon him. May I never meet with trouble in life.

O Grandfather, chief of the Thunderbirds, you who live in the west, here is a handful of tobacco. Extend to me the deer with which you blessed my ancestor. I pray to accept this tobacco from me. May I never meet with trouble in life.

O Grandfathers, spirits of the night, walkers in darkness, to you I offer tobacco and ask for the fireplaces which my ancestor received. If you smoke this tobacco see to it that I never become a weakling.

To you who live in the south, you who look like a man, you who are invulnerable, you who deal out life from one side of your body and death from the other, you whom we call Disease Giver, to you I offer tobacco. In daylight, in broad daylight, did you bless my ancestor. With food you blessed him; you told him that he would never fail in anything, you told him that you would avoid his home; you placed animals in front of him that he should have no trouble in obtaining them. An offering of tobacco I make to you that you may smoke it and that I may not be troubled in life.

From *ibid.*, pp. 80-1.

THE SENECA CHIEF RED JACKET ADDRESSES A MISSIONARY ON A COUNCIL HELD AT BUFFALO IN THE YEAR 1805

[After the missionary had done speaking, the Indians conferred together about two hours, by themselves, when they gave an answer by Red Jacket, which follows:]

Friend and brother, it was the will of the Great Spirit that we should meet together this day. He orders all things, and he has given us a fine day for our council. He has taken his garment from before the sun, and caused it to shine with brightness upon us; our eyes are opened, that we see clearly; our ears are unstopped, that we have been able to hear distinctly the words that you have spoken; for all these favors we thank the Great Spirit, and him only.

Brother, this council fire was kindled by you; it was at your request that we came together at this time; we have listened with attention to what you have said; you requested us to speak our minds freely; this gives us great joy, for we now consider that we stand upright before you, and can speak what we think; all have heard your voice, and all speak to you as one man; our minds are agreed.

Brother, you say you want an answer to your talk before you leave this place. It is right you should have one, as you are a great distance from home, and we do not wish to detain you; but we will first look back a little, and tell you what our fathers have told us, and what we have heard from the white people.

Brother, listen to what we say. There was a time when our forefathers owned this great island. Their seats extended from the rising to the setting sun. The Great Spirit had made it for the use of the Indians. He had created the buffalo, the deer, and other animals for food. He made the bear and the beaver, and their skins served us for clothing. He had scattered them over the country, and taught us how to take them. He had caused the earth to produce corn for bread. All this he had done for his red children because he loved them. If we had any disputes about hunting grounds, they were generally settled without the shedding of much blood: but an evil day came upon us; your forefathers crossed the great waters and landed on this island. Their numbers were small; they found friends, not enemies; they told us they had fled from their own country for fear of wicked men, and come here to enjoy their religion. They asked for a small seat; we took pity on them, granted their request, and they sat down among us; we gave them corn and meat; they gave us poison in return. The white people had now found our country, tidings were carried back, and more came among us; yet we did not fear them, we took them to be friends; they called us brothers; we believed them and gave them a larger seat. At length their number had greatly increased; they wanted more land; they wanted our country. Our eyes were opened, and our minds became uneasy. Wars took place; Indians were hired to fight against Indians, and many of our people were destroyed. They also brought strong liquors among us: it was strong and powerful, and has slain thousands.

Brother, our seats were once large, and yours were

very small; you have now become a great people, and we have scarcely left a place to spread our blankets; you have got our country, but are not satisfied; you want to force your religion upon us.

Brother, continue to listen. You say that you are sent to instruct us how to worship the Great Spirit agreeably to his mind, and if we do not take hold of the religion which you white people teach, we shall be unhappy hereafter; you say that you are right, and we are lost; how do we know this to be true? We understand that your religion is written in a book; if it was intended for us as well as you, why has not the Great Spirit given it to us, and not only to us, but why did he not give to our forefathers the knowledge of that book, with the means of understanding it rightly? We only know what you tell us about it; how shall we know when to believe, being so often deceived by the white people?

Brother, you say there is but one way to worship and serve the Great Spirit; if there is but one religion, why do you white people differ so much about it? Why do not all agree, as you can all read the book?

Brother, we do not understand these things; we are told that your religion was given to your forefathers, and has been handed down from father to son. We also have a religion which was given to our forefathers, and has been handed down to us their children. We worship that way. It teacheth us to be thankful for all the favors we receive; to love each other, and to be united. We never quarrel about religion.

Brother, the Great Spirit has made us all; but he has made a great difference between his white and red children; he has given us a different complexion, and different customs; to you he has given the arts; to these he has not opened our eyes; we know these things to be true. Since he has made so great a difference between us in other things, why may we not conclude that he has given us a different religion according to our understanding; the Great Spirit does right; he knows what is best for his children; we are satisfied.

Brother, we do not wish to destroy your religion, or take it from you; we only want to enjoy our own.

Brother, you say you have not come to get our land or our money, but to enlighten our minds. I will now tell you that I have been at your meetings, and saw you collecting money from the meeting. I cannot tell what this money was intended for, but suppose it was for your minister, and if we should conform to your way of thinking, perhaps you may want some from us.

Brother, we are told that you have been preaching to white people in this place; these people are our neighbors, we are acquainted with them; we will wait a little while and see what effect your preaching has upon them. If we find it does them good, makes them honest, and less disposed to cheat Indians, we will then consider again what you have said.

Brother, you have now heard the answer to your talk, and this is all we have to say at present. As we are going to part, we will come and take you by the hand, and hope the Great Spirit will protect you on your journey, and return you safe to your friends.

From Samuel G. Drake, *Biography and History of the Indians of North America*, pp. 594 ff. This speech, says Drake, may be taken as genuine, at least as nearly so as the

Indian language in which it was delivered can be translated, for Red Jacket would not speak in English, although he understood it. After the Seneca chief had finished his speech, he and others drew near the missionary to take him by the hand; but he would not receive them, and, hastily rising from his seat, said "that there was no fellowship between the religion of God and the works of the devil, therefore, could not join hands with them." The Indians withdrew—politely smiling.

FROM THE BIG HOUSE CEREMONY
(Delaware)

[The Speaker calls upon the Spirit Forces:]

"Truly we are thankful that we have lived long enough to see the time come when these our grandfathers the trees bloom forth, and also the coming up of vegetation.

"Now as well for this water and for him our grandfather fire, and again this air, again this sunlight. When everyone has been blessed with such gifts it is enough to make one realise what kind of benevolence comes from our father, because he it is who has created everything."

[The Narrator tells about the First Night of the Ceremony:]

The Master of Ceremony says when he goes into the Big House, when rising to his feet, he speaks saying, "Truly I am thankful, my kindred. It is exceedingly good that we have lived on through to see each other, that we are in good health. I am truly thankful to bring forth the blessing, my brothers and sisters and those there, our children. I bless you all with every kind of blessing. Truly it is unbecoming to me because I feel incompetent when instructing you what to do. Pitiful am I, indeed, as it is said. It rests very heavily upon my mind when I see each year how at present this our way of living has become pitiful. But nevertheless we must all try, my brothers and sisters and also even those children. Let everyone use his mind earnestly when we lift up our prayer of appeal to that one, our father, the Great Spirit and Our Creator. Indeed, it is with great sadness of mind that we look back and see the past of our cultural life as it is said to have been. . . . Indeed, it brings sadness of mind when we see here now how few of our relatives are seated around that space. It is enough to make anyone ponder over the cause of it. I myself never did think that I would live long enough, as a survivor, living as I am right here instructing in sacred things where other sacred teachers, our deceased ancestors, so thoroughly inspired in worship, taught. So I pray that everyone help. If accordingly everyone does all in his power, earnestly praying with all his heart, it might occasion those spirit forces to hear our pitiful appeal, those who carry the power of blessing. And right here this evening in a little while we shall begin to feel ourselves being touched by our grandfathers who move this our prayer-worship." . . .[1]

[And the Narrator continues:]

"I am truly thankful that I bring the address of blessing, my brothers, my sisters, and these our children. I give thanks that I bring blessing, all and every kind of spiritual blessings. Truly I am very feeble myself, as it is said, it oppresses my heart when I see how now we are orphans. Many times we have heard from our deceased ancestors how, so it is said, they sadly pleaded, when, reciting their vision experience, telling how pitiful were the conditions then in their time said to be. Verily I myself do grieve, my kindred, when I look back there into the past. But, nevertheless, indeed try your utmost, everyone have a helpful will,

[1] Follows Recitation of Vision.

167

and it might be that our pitiful plea for mercy be heard by him the Great Spirit. We may perchance sometime gain a victory to our benefit.

"Truly, my kindred, as it is forcibly said, I am oppressed with a feeling of incapability while standing here to instruct anyone in the blessing, here where stands he our Grandfather.[2] And I am truly thankful to bless with gratitude all those spirit forces, all of them sitting round about us over the entire earth. And when we consider how our deceased ancestors so thoroughly paid attention to the obligations of this prayer-worship! Indeed how greatly are we privileged and blessed that still we can perform the ceremony as we were accustomed to see our deceased ancestors do it! This is sufficient for this occasion. Thanks!"[3]

[The Master of Ceremonies addresses the assemblage on the morning of the Thirteenth Day:]

"My kindred, there remains one more matter, something I want to say for you to bear well in mind. It is said traditionally, when anyone on Good meditates in his heart, there is formed the thought. And when he thinks of Good it is easy to behave well, but when he misbehaves it is the Evil that a person seriously thinks about as concerns his life. It is exceedingly hard because it is necessary that we prepare the soul-spirit in order that we shall be able to take it back

[2] He refers to the carved image of the Great Spirit on the central post of the Big House.

[3] The ceremony proper lasts 12 days. The most conspicuous features of this ritual are the recitations of visions, always followed by a dance down the White Path, the ceremonial eating of hominy, the kindling of the new fire, and the burning of the sacred cedar.

168

home again to where it belongs, to our father, when its use is finished here where we live. Here in this place it is the body that shall remain here because here is where it belongs in the ground. . . .

"And now, my kindred, here when for the last time we are touched by these our grandfathers the turtle-rattles, that is the beginning of our concluding act. Now here at last we are ready to end this our father's service. And, my kindred, now from hence as we are going home, you must take good care, for you are carrying with you the spirit of Delaware worship." . . .

From Frank G. Speck, *A Study of the Delaware Indian Big House Ceremony.* In native text dictated by Witapanóxwe. Pp. 105, 113, 115, 125, 127, 161, 163. One understands best the intrinsic meaning of the Big House Ceremony by going somewhat into the concept of the White Path. As most of the "temples" the world over, the Big House of the Delaware Indians—a tribe belonging to the Algonquian stock—symbolizes the universe. The White Path is the hard-trodden dancing path outlined on the floor of the Big House winding from the east door down toward the north, passing around the two sacred fires, and again around the center post, upon which the image of the highest manitou is carved, doubling back to the south and from there to the west door, the exit, the place of sunset where all things end. The White Path is the symbol of the transit of life; it stands for the road of life down which man wends his way with iron inevitability. But it also stands, according to Frank Speck, for the journey of the soul after death, for it corresponds to the Milky Way, the path of the souls.

This ceremony, then, is not only one that is thought to serve general purification, but also to promote life and health, and, above all, to strengthen the bonds with the ancestors, one of the main prerequisites to increasing the powers of life. Pp. 22-3.

LAMENTATION

(IROQUOIS)

I come again to greet and thank the League;
I come again to greet and thank the kindred;
I come again to greet and thank the warriors;
I come again to greet and thank the women.
My forefathers,—what they established,—
My forefathers,—hearken to them!

A-haigh, my grandsires! Now hearken while your grandchildren cry mournfully to you, because the Great League which you established has grown old. We hope that they may hear.

A-haigh, my grandsires! You have said that sad will be the fate of those who come in the latter times.

O, my grandsires! Even now I may have failed to perform this ceremony in the order in which they were wont to perform it.

O, my grandsires! Even now that has become old which you established—the Great League. You have it as a pillow under your heads in the ground where you are lying—this Great League which you established; although you said that far away in the future the Great League would endure.

Now listen, ye who established the Great League. Now it has become old. Now there is nothing but wilderness. Ye are in your graves who established it. Ye have taken it with you, and have placed it under you, and there is nothing left but a desert. There ye have taken your intellects with you. What ye established—the Great League.

From Horatio Hale, *The Iroquois Book of Rites,* pp. 123, 129. In every important council of the Iroquois a song or chant was considered one of the most essential parts of the proceedings. In the Rite of the Condoling Council, which is the greatest of all councils and which presents the lamentation for a departed chief of the Great League and the installation of a new chief, the preceding hymn must be of especial significance. The above hymn is taken from the Canienga version of the Book of Rites and offers the solemn introduction to the equally important ceremony which is to follow—that is, the repetition of the ancient laws of the Iroquois Confederacy. As a whole, says Hale, this hymn, which is of considerable antiquity, may be considered as an expression of reverence for the laws and for the dead, and of sympathy for the living, p. 64.

SECTION TWO:

From the Southeast

FORMULA TO ATTRACT AFFECTIONS
(CHEROKEE)

Kû! Listen! In Alahíyi you repose, O Terrible Woman.
Oh, you have drawn near to hearken.
There in Alahíyi you are at rest, O White Woman.
No one is ever lonely when with you.
You are most beautiful.
Instantly and at once you have rendered me a white
   man.
No one is ever lonely when with me.
Now you have made the path white for me.
I shall never be dreary. . . .
I shall never become blue.
You have brought down to me the white road.
There in midearth you have placed me.
I shall stand erect upon the earth.
No one is ever lonely when with me.
I am very handsome. You have put me into the white
   house.
I shall be in it as it moves about
And no one with me shall ever be lonely.
Verily, I shall never become blue.
Instantly you have caused it to be so with me.

And now there in Alahíyi you have rendered the
   woman blue.
Now you have made the path blue for her;
Let her be completely veiled in loneliness.
Put her into the blue road.
And now bring her down.
Place her standing upon the earth.

Where her feet are now and wherever she may go,
Let loneliness leave its mark upon her.
Let her be marked out for loneliness where she stands.

Ha! I belong to the Wolf clan,
That one alone which was alotted for you.
No one is ever lonely with me. I am handsome.
Let her put her soul
Into the very center of my soul, never to turn away.
Grant that in the midst of men
She shall never think of them.
I belong to the one clan alone which was allotted for
    you
When the seven clans were established.

Where [other] men live it is lonely.
They are very loathsome.
The common polecat has made them so like himself
That they are fit only for his company.
They have become mere refuse.
They are very loathsome.
The common oppossum has made them so like himself
That they are fit only to be with him.
They are very loathsome.
Even the crow has made them so like himself
That they are fit only for his company.
They are very loathsome.
The miserable rain-crow has made them so like himself
That they are fit only to be with him.

The seven clans all alike make one feel lonely in their
    company.
They are not even good looking.
They go about clothed with mere refuse.

They go about even covered with dung.
But I—I was ordained to be a white man.
I stand with my face toward the Sun Land.
No one is ever lonely with me. I am very handsome.
I shall certainly never become blue.
I am covered with the everlasting white house
Wherever I go.
No one is ever lonely with me.
Your soul has come into the very center of my soul,
Never to turn away.
I, Gatigwanasti, I take your soul. *Sgé!*

From James Mooney, *Sacred Formulas of the Cherokees,*
pp. 376-7. Mooney obtained a number of sacred formulas
on the Cherokee Reservation in North Carolina. These
formulas, covering every subject pertaining to the daily
life and thought of the Indian, including medicine, love,
hunting, war, etc., were written by the shamans of the tribe,
for their own use, in the Cherokee characters invented by
Sequoyah in 1821, and were obtained with explanations,
either from the writers themselves or from their surviving
relatives. The above Love Charm appears to be recited by
the lover himself—not by a shaman. Blue is the color of
distress, white that of happiness.

FORMULA TO DESTROY LIFE
(Cherokee)

Listen! Now I have come to step over your soul.
You are of the wolf clan. Your name is Áyûiuni.
Your spittle I have put at rest under the earth.
Your soul I have put at rest under the earth.
I have come to cover you over with the black rock.
I have come to cover you with the black slabs, never
    to reappear.
Toward the black coffin in the Darkening Land your
    path shall stretch out.
So shall it be for you.
The clay of the upland has come [to cover you].
Instantly the black clay has lodged there where it is
    at rest at the black houses in the Darkening Land.
With the black coffin and the black slabs I have come
    to cover you.
Now your soul has faded away.
It has become blue.
When darkness comes
Your spirit shall grow less
And dwindle away,
Never to reappear. Listen!

From *ibid.,* p. 391.

178

ORIGIN OF THE PLEIADES AND THE PINE

(CHEROKEE)

Long ago, when the world was new, there were seven boys who used to spend all their time down by the townshouse playing the *gatayŭ'sti* game, rolling a stone wheel along the ground and sliding a curved stick after it to strike it. Their mothers scolded, but it did no good, so one day they collected *gatayŭ'sti* stones and boiled them in the pot with the corn for dinner. When the boys came home hungry their mothers dipped out the stones and said, "Since you like the *gatayŭ'sti* stones better than the cornfields, take the stones now for your dinner."

The boys were very angry, and went down to the townshouse saying, "As our mothers treat us that way, let us go where we shall never trouble them any more." They began a dance—some say it was the Feather Dance—and went round and round the townshouse, praying to the spirits to help them. At last their mothers were afraid something was wrong and went out to look for them. They saw the boys still dancing around the townshouse, and as they watched they noticed that their feet were off the earth, and that with every round they rose higher and higher in the air. They ran to get their children, but it was too late, for they were already above the roof of the townshouse— all but one, whose mother managed to pull him down with the *gatayŭ'sti* pole, but he struck the ground with such a force that he sank into it and the earth closed over him.

The other six circled higher and higher until they went up to the sky, where we see them now as the Pleiades, which the Cherokee still call *Anitsutsa*, the Boys. The people grieved long after them, but the mother whose boy had gone into the ground came every morning and every evening to cry over the spot until the earth was damp with her tears. At last a little green shoot sprouted up and grew day by day until it became the tall tree that we call now the pine, and the pine is of the same nature as the stars and holds in itself the same bright light.

From James Mooney, *Myths of the Cherokees,* p. 258.

SECTION THREE:

From the Deserts of the Southwest

THE WAR GOD'S HORSE SONG
(NAVAJO)

I am the Turquoise Woman's son.
On top of Belted Mountain
Beautiful horses—slim like a weasel!
My horse has a hoof like striped agate;
His fetlock is like a fine eagle plume;
His legs are like quick lightning.
My horse's body is like an eagle-plumed arrow;
My horse has a tail like a trailing black cloud.
I put flexible goods on my horse's back;
The Little Holy Wind blows through his hair.

His mane is made of short rainbows.
My horse's ears are made of round corn.
My horse's eyes are made of big stars.
My horse's head is made of mixed waters
(From the holy waters—he never knows thirst).
My horse's teeth are made of white shell.
The long rainbow is in his mouth for a bridle,
    And with it I guide him.
When my horse neighs, different-colored horses follow.
When my horse neighs, different-colored sheep follow.
    I am wealthy, because of him.

    Before me peaceful,
    Behind me peaceful,
    Under me peaceful,
    Over me peaceful,
    All around me peaceful—
    Peaceful voice when he neighs.

183

I am Everlasting and Peaceful.
I stand for my horse.

From Dane and Mary Roberts Coolidge, *The Navajo Indians*, p. 2. Living now in the semi-arid desert regions of the southwest, the Navajo are mainly herdsmen, skillful blanket weavers, and unexcelled silversmiths. Their unusually poetical cycles of songs breathe the infiniteness of the sky, and their melodies are carried by the soft warm smell of the unbroken soil. The resemblance of certain traits of Navajo myth and song with epic and song of the south Siberian tribes is striking.

A PRAYER OF THE NIGHT CHANT

(NAVAJO)

Tségihi.
House made of dawn.
House made of evening light.
House made of the dark cloud.
House made of male rain.
House made of dark mist.
House made of female rain.
House made of pollen.
House made of grasshoppers.
Dark cloud is at the door.
The trail out of it is dark cloud.
The zigzag lightning stands high upon it.
Male deity!
Your offering I make.
I have prepared a smoke for you.
Restore my feet for me.
Restore my legs for me.
Restore my body for me.
Restore my mind for me.
This very day take out your spell for me.
Your spell remove for me.
You have taken it away for me.
Far off it has gone.
Happily I recover.
Happily my interior becomes cool.
Happily I go forth.
My interior feeling cool, may I walk.
No longer sore, may I walk.

Impervious to pain, may I walk.
With lively feelings may I walk.
As it used to be long ago, may I walk.
Happily may I walk.
Happily, with abundant dark clouds, may I walk.
Happily, with abundant showers, may I walk.
Happily, with abundant plants, may I walk.
Happily, on a trail of pollen, may I walk.
Happily may I walk.
Being as it used to be long ago, may I walk.
May it be beautiful before me.
May it be beautiful behind me.
May it be beautiful below me.
May it be beautiful above me.
May it be beautiful all around me.
In beauty it is finished.

From Washington Matthews, *Navajo Myths, Prayers, and Songs*, pp. 54-5.

SONG OF THE BLACK BEAR

(NAVAJO)

My moccasins are black obsidian,
My leggings are black obsidian,
My shirt is black obsidian.
I am girded with a black arrowsnake.
Black snakes go up from my head.
With zigzag lightning darting from the ends of my
    feet I step,
With zigzag lightning streaming out from my knees
    I step,
With zigzag lightning streaming from the tip of my
    tongue I speak.
Now a disk of pollen rests on the crown of my head.
Gray arrowsnakes and rattlesnakes eat it.
Black obsidian and zigzag lightning streams out from
    me in four ways,
Where they strike the earth, bad things, bad talk does
    not like it.
It causes the missiles to spread out.
Long Life, something frightful I am.
Now I am.

There is danger where I move my feet.
I am whirlwind.
There is danger when I move my feet.
I am a gray bear.
When I walk, where I step, lightning flies from me,
Where I walk, one to be feared [I am].

Where I walk, Long Life.
One to be feared I am.
There is danger where I walk.

From Pliny Earle Goddard, *Navajo Texts*, pp. 176, 178.

BIRTH OF WHITE SHELL WOMAN
(NAVAJO)

Times were hard in the world. Everywhere there were beings who were eating people. One day a dark rain cloud was seen resting on top of Tc'ol'i. The next day the rain was seen to be falling nearly to the middle of the mountain. The third day it reached well beyond the middle, and the fourth day the rain enveloped the entire mountain and was falling at its base.

First Man, observing this from the top of Dzilna' oditi, addressing First Woman, said, "Old Woman, four days ago there was a dark rain cloud on the top of Tc'ol'i, and now the entire mountain is covered with rain. Something unusual has happened. I am going to see what it is." "There are things to be feared there. The devouring ones are many. Why do you go?" First Woman replied. "Nothing untoward will happen," First Man said and started away on a run. When he had run some distance he began to sing:

"I am approaching, close I am approaching.
I being associated with the dawn, First Man I am.
Now the mountain Tc'ol'i I am approaching.
Where it is black with rain clouds I am
    approaching.
Where the zigzag lightning lies above I am
    approaching.
Where the rainbow lies above I am approaching.
Where it is murky with the abounding water I am
    approaching.

Possessed of long life and good fortune I am approaching.
With good fortune before me,
With good fortune behind me,
With good fortune under me,
With good fortune above me,
With good fortune all around me,
With good fortune proceeding from my mouth I come to it."

. . . When First Man came to the top of the mountain he heard a baby crying. The lightning striking all about and murk caused by the hard rain made it difficult to see anything. He discovered the baby lying with its head towards the west and its feet towards the east. Its cradle consisted of two short rainbows which lay longitudinally under it. Crosswise, at its chest and feet, lay red rays of the rising sun. Arched over its face was a rainbow. The baby was wrapped in four blankets—dark cloud, blue cloud, yellow cloud, and white cloud. Along either side was a row of loops made of lightning and through these a sunbeam was laced back and forth.

First Man, not knowing how to undo the fastenings, took up the baby, cradle and all, and started home. . . . When he arrived he called out, "Old Woman, it is a baby, I found it there where it is black night with rain clouds." He put the baby on the ground back of the fire, pulled the string, and the lacing came free in both directions. "The cradle shall be like this. Thin pieces of wood shall be placed underneath. There will be a row of loops on either side made of string. The bark of the cliff rose, shredded and rubbed fine, will be used under the child for a bed." It was a girl. . . .

A day was the same as a year. The second day the girl sat up, and when two days had passed she looked around. And when three days had passed she danced. . . . And on the tenth day, at dawn, she was named Yolkai Estsan, White Shell Woman.

From *ibid.*, pp. 148-50. The highest place in the Navajo pantheon is held by Estsanatlehi, the Woman Who Changes —for she has the gift of renewing herself whenever she grows old. Her younger sister is Yolkai Estsan, the White Shell Woman. The white shell is her symbol; white is the color of dawn and the east, and she is related to the waters. She was to become the wife of the Moon-Carrier, Klehanoai.

RAIN SONG
(Pima)

Hi-iya naiho-o! The earth is rumbling
From the beating of our basket drums.
The earth is rumbling from the beating
Of our basket drums, everywhere humming.
Earth is rumbling, everywhere raining.

Hi-iya naiho-o! Pluck out the feathers
    From the wing of the eagle and turn them
Toward the east where lie the large clouds.
    Hi-iya naiho-o! Pluck out the soft down
From the breast of the eagle and turn it
    Toward the west where sail the small clouds.
Hi-iya naiho-o! Beneath the abode
    Of the rain gods it is thundering;
Large corn is there. *Hi-iya naiho-o!*
    Beneath the abode of the rain gods
It is raining; small corn is there.

From Frank Russel, *The Pima Indians,* p. 332. The
singing of this song is supposed to provoke rain. The sound
of the basket drum urges the clouds to gather and the thun-
der to rumble beneath the sky. The eagle down symbolizes
clouds, its offering to the quarters makes the clouds drift
in the wished-for direction.

WAR SONG

(Papago)

Is it for me to eat what food I have
And all day sit idle?
Is it for me to drink the sweet water poured out
And all day sit idle?
Is it for me to gaze upon my wife
And all day sit idle?
Is it for me to hold my child in my arms
And all day sit idle?

My desire was uncontrollable.
It was the dizziness [of battle];
I ground it to powder and therewith I painted my face.
It was the drunkenness of battle;
I ground it to powder and therewith I tied my hair
  in a war knot.
Then did I hold firm my well-strung bow and my
  smooth, straight-flying arrow.
To me did I draw my far-striding sandals, and fast I
  tied them.

Over the flat land did I then go striding,
Over the embedded stones did I then go stumbling,
Under the trees in the ditches did I go stooping,
Through the trees on the high ground did I go
  hurtling,
Through the mountain gullies did I go brushing
  quickly.

In four halts did I reach the shining white eagle,
  my guardian,

And I asked power.
Then favorable to me he felt
And did bring forth his shining white stone.
Our enemy's mountain he made white as with
    moonlight
And brought them close,
And across them I went striding.

In four halts did I reach the blue hawk, my
    guardian,
And I asked power.
The hawk favorable to me he felt
And did bring forth his blue stone.
Our enemy's waters he made white as with moonlight,
And around them I went striding.
There did I seize and pull up and make into a bundle
Those things which were my enemy's,
All kinds of seeds and beautiful clouds and beautiful
    winds.

Then came forth a thick stalk and a thick tassel,
And the undying seed did ripen.
This I did on behalf of my people.
Thus should you also think and desire,
All you my kinsmen.

From Ruth Underhill, *Singing for Power, the Song Magic of the Papago Indians of Southern Arizona*, pp. 68-9. A delightful little volume that should be in the hands of everybody who wishes to gain some insight into the Indian's mentality.

DREAM SONG OF A WOMAN
(PAPAGO)

Where the mountain crosses,
On top of the mountain,
   I do not myself know where.
I wandered where my mind and my heart
   seemed to be lost.
I wandered away.

From Frances Densmore, *Papago Music,* p. 206.

DEATH SONG
(Papago)

In the great night my heart will go out.
Toward me the darkness comes rattling,
In the great night my heart will go out.

From *ibid.*, p. 126. A song of Owl Woman.

196

CEREMONIAL SUN SONG
(Papago)

In the east is the dwelling of the sun.
On top of this dwelling place
The sun comes up and travels over our heads.
Below we travel.
I raise my right hand to the sun
And then stroke my body
In the ceremonial manner.

From *ibid.*, p. 137. This song belongs to a Dance in Supplication to the Sun.

TWO RAIN SONGS
(Papago)

1.

Close to the west the great ocean is singing.
The waves are rolling toward me, covered with
   many clouds.
Even here I catch the sound.
The earth is shaking beneath me and I hear the
   deep rumbling.

2.

A cloud on top of Evergreen Mountain is singing,
A cloud on top of Evergreen Mountain is
   standing still,
It is raining and thundering up there,
It is raining here,
Under the mountain the corn tassels are shaking,
Under the mountain the horns of the child corn
   are glistening.

From *ibid.*, pp. 140-1. Songs of the Viikita Ceremony,
performed in order to secure rain and good crops.

FROM THE AUTOBIOGRAPHY OF A PAPAGO WOMAN

1.

On winter nights, when we had finished our gruel or rabbit stew and lay back on our mats, my brothers would say to my father: "My father, tell us something."

My father would lie quietly upon his mat with my mother beside him and the baby between them. At last he would start slowly to tell us about how the world began. This is a story that can be told only in winter when there are no snakes about, for if the snakes heard they could crawl in and bite you. But in winter when snakes are asleep, we tell these things. Our story about the world is full of songs, and when the neighbors heard my father singing they would open our door and step in over the high threshold. Family by family they came, and we made a big fire and kept the door shut against the cold night. When my father finished a sentence we would all say the last word after him. If anyone went to sleep he would stop. He would not speak any more. But we did not go to sleep. . . .

My father was a song maker, and he had visions even if he was not a medicine man. He always made a song for the big harvest festival, the one that keeps the world going right and that only comes every four years.

We all went then from all over our country to the Place of the Burnt Seeds. We camped together, many,

many families, and we made images of the beautiful things that make life good for the desert people, like clouds and corn and squash and deer. The men sang about these things and my father made songs. When I was about eight years old, my father once made an image of a mountain out of cactus ribs covered with white cloth. He had dreamed about this mountain and this is the song he made:

> There is a white shell mountain in the ocean
> Rising half out of the water.
> Green scum floats on the water
> And the mountain turns around.

The song is very short because we understand so much. We can understand how tall and white the mountain was, and that white shell is something precious, such as the handsome men of old used to have for their necklaces, and it would shine all across the earth as they walked. We understand that as that mountain turns, it draws the clouds and the birds until they all float around it.

2.

At last the giant cactus grew ripe on all the hills. It made us laugh to see the fruit on top of all the stalks. . . . We went to pick it, to the same place where we always camped, and every day my mother and all the women went out with baskets. They knocked the fruit down with cactus poles. It fell on the ground and all the red pulp came out. Then I picked it up and dug it out of the shell with my fingers, and put it in my mother's basket. She told me always to throw down the skins with the red inside uppermost, because that would bring the rain.

It was good at cactus camp. When my father lay down to sleep at night he would sing a song about the cactus liquor. And we could hear songs in my uncle's camp across the hill. Everybody sang. We felt as if a beautiful thing was coming. Because the rain was coming and the dancing and the songs.

> Where on Quijota Mountain a cloud stands
> There my heart stands with it.
> Where the mountain trembles with the thunder
> My heart trembles with it.

That was what they sang. When I sing that song yet it makes me dance.

Then the little rains began to come. We had jugs of the juice my mother had boiled. . . . And we drank it to pull down the clouds, for that is what we call it.

From R. Underhill, *The Autobiography of a Papago Woman,* pp. 10-1, 22-3.

SONG TO PULL DOWN THE CLOUDS
(Papago)

At the edge of the world
It is growing light.
Up rears the light.
Just yonder the day dawns,
Spreading over the night.

From Ruth Underhill, *Singing for Power,* p. 27. "Song
was not simply self-expression. It was a magic which called
upon the powers of Nature and constrained them to man's
will. People sang in trouble, in danger, to cure the sick, to
confound their enemies, and to make the crops grow." p. 5.

A PRAYER

(HAVASUPAI)

Sun, my relative
Be good coming out
Do something good for us.

Make me work,
So I can do anything in the garden
I hoe, I plant corn, I irrigate.

You, sun, be good going down at sunset
We lay down to sleep I want to feel good.

While I sleep you come up.
Go on your course many times.
Make good things for us men.

Make me always the same as I am now.

This literal translation is from Leslie Spier, *Havasupai Ethnography,* p. 286.

THE POWER THAT FAILED

(Chiricahua)

My father once cured me with his ceremony. I was a pretty small boy. I can hardly remember it. My father says that I must have been about six years old. . . .

I got very, very sick. My mother and my father thought I was going to die. This was out in the mountains. Of course, my father knew in his own way how to use his power and cure people. So my father went to work on me during part of the day and a good part of the night, I know. While he was carrying on the ceremony for me, I went blind, completely blind.

Well, he got me a little better from my sickness, but after I got well I was blind. It seemed as though my eyes were back in my head, and they hurt badly. It looked as though a different sickness had come over my eyes. It was just as though something was turning way back in my head.

My father was very good at the masked-dancer ceremony. . . .

He had the mask in his right hand and was shaking it in front of me. He was singing those ceremonial songs. Every time he sang a song he held that mask to my head this way and that, to my eyes and all over me. I was half-sitting up, on a slant. I couldn't see, but I knew what he was doing and what he was saying. I remember it.

And my father was crying half of the time; I could hear him. He said, "Why not punish me this way? I've lived here many years on earth. I've seen what it looks like. I know how hard it is to live through this world. Don't kill that poor little child. He didn't harm anyone. I love him. Don't let him go. I want him to live to an old age in this world." He said, "If you want to kill anybody in this family, kill me. Take me. I know you can help me relieve this poor child from his sickness, and there's no reason why you should act this way to me." He was angry about this, angry at his own power. I heard him arguing with his power. He tried pretty hard. "Well," he said to his power, "if you aren't going to do what I want you to do, if you're going to have your own way all the time, you might as well stop talking to me from now on." He was scolding his power. . . .

From Morris Edward Opler, *An Apache Life Way, The Economic, Social, and Religious Institutions of the Chiricahua Indians.* p. 39. On the whole, the problem of the Theodicy did not exist for the Indian. He did not believe in an all-powerful God who, single-handedly, had created earth and man. Therefore he had not to rack his head as to how to reconcile the idea of a good and omnipotent God with the evil in the world. However, here and there we find traces of this problem in its incipient stage as, for instance, in the story above. Compare also the passionate account of the Fox Indian who reproaches the manitou (page 149). Another example is given by Frances Densmore, who recorded the death song of a Sioux: in the hour of his death he becomes aware that his guardian spirit had misguided him, and thus he sings sadly with his last strength:
"Large Bear
Deceives me." *(Chippewa Music II, p. 80.)*

SONGS OF MATURATION

Sung during the Girls' Puberty Rites
(CHIRICAHUA)

1.

I come to White Painted Woman,
By means of long life I come to her.
I come to her by means of her blessing,
I come to her by means of her good fortune,
I come to her by means of all her different fruits.
By means of the long life she bestows, I come
    to her.
By means of this holy truth she goes about.

2.

I am about to sing this song of yours,
The song of long life.
Sun, I stand here on the earth with your song,
Moon, I have come in with your song.

3.

White Painted Woman's power emerges,
Her power for sleep.
White Painted Woman carries this girl;
She carries her through long life,
She carries her to good fortune,
She carries her to old age,
She bears her to peaceful sleep.

4.

You have started out on the good earth;
You have started out with good moccasins;
With moccasin strings of the rainbow, you have
started out.
With moccasin strings of the sun rays, you have
started out.
In the midst of plenty you have started out.

From *ibid.*, pp. 119, 128, 130. The Puberty Ceremony for Girls, as performed by the Chiricahua and led by the Masked Dancers, is, essentially, a prayer for long life—and in order to obtain this blessing of all blessings, songs are sung over the girl which first are to conduct her to the "holy home" and from there symbolically through a long and successful life. The ceremony lasts four nights and is concluded in the face of the rising sun of the fifth day with Song 4, "a graceful apotheosis of the life-journey upon which the adolescent girl has embarked." White Painted Woman is associated with earth and is the power that symbolizes the feminine principle.

TWO LOVE SONGS
(CHIRICAHUA)

1.

Maiden, you talk kindly to me,
    You, I shall surely remember it,
I shall surely remember you alone,
Your words are so kind,
    You, I shall surely remember it.

2.

My sweetheart, we surely could have gone home,
But you were afraid!
When it was night we surely could have gone
    home,
But you were afraid!

From *ibid.*, p. 125. Toward morning of the first three nights of the Puberty Rite for girls the sacred songs change into social ones. The songs of the third dawn may be called true love songs, and one of the informants said to Opler: "We like them best of all. People just fall in love there singing them."

PRAYER AFTER SINGING GAHÉ SONGS
(CHIRICAHUA)

Big Blue Mountain Spirit,
The home made of blue clouds,
The cross made of the blue mirage,
There, you have begun to live,
There, is the life of goodness,
I am grateful for that made of goodness there.

Big Yellow Mountain Spirit in the south,
Your spiritually hale body is made of yellow clouds;
Leader of the Mountain Spirits, holy Mountain Spirit,
You live by means of the good of this life.

Big White Mountain Spirit in the west,
Your spiritually hale body is made of the white mirage;
Holy Mountain Spirit, leader of the Mountain Spirits,
I am happy over your words,
You are happy over my words.

Big Black Mountain Spirit in the north,
Your spiritually hale body is made of black clouds;
In that way, Big Black Mountain Spirit,
Holy Mountain Spirit, leader of the Mountain Spirits,
I am happy over your words,
You are happy over my words,
Now it is good.

From Harry Hoijer, *Chiricahua and Mescalero Apache Texts,* p. 69. The Mountain Spirits are supernaturals who dwell within the interior of the mountains, where they live a life much as the Apache used to do in aboriginal times. Some of the Mountain Spirits appear as the Masked Dancers *(gahé)* during the adolescence ceremonies for girls; they also cure and punish. The prayer given above indicates the happy fellowship that exists between the supernaturals and the shaman. It is the "word" that re-establishes the rapport between the spirit and the human being and expresses to perfection their reciprocal need. See Ethnographical Notes, pp. 143, 155. This creative comradeship between deity and man is expressed still more distinctly in another song:

> "He performs the ceremony with me;
> The ceremony has begun with me;
> He is happy over me, I am happy over him;
> My songs will go out . . ."

THE MOUNTAIN SPIRITS AND THE
OLD WOMAN
(CHIRICAHUA)

Long ago, the Indians were traveling. And some old woman was among them. And it seems they did not like her.

Then it seems they spoke thus: "This old woman is good for nothing," they said. Then they had spoken thus. "This old woman is good for nothing," they said; "therefore, let's abandon her," they said. Then they had abandoned her.

Then it seems she wept. Then these Mountain Spirits came to her. And they spoke thus to her: "Why are you weeping?" they said to her.

"I weep because they have abandoned me," she said. "I cannot see, I cannot hear, and I cannot speak. For that reason, I weep."

Then they began to sing for her. And she who had been blind, her eyes were made to open. She who had been deaf began to hear again. She who had been blind was made to see again.

Then they spoke thus to her: "This that we have done is good. When you return, tell them about it," they said to her.

Then she performed all of the ceremony they had done for her in exactly their way. And in that way she returned.

Then she performed all of that which had been given to her in exactly their way. And, in this way, the ceremony came to be customarily performed.

From *ibid.*, p. 33. This text—the translation of which is

211

as literal as could be—is, from an ethnological point of view, interesting in several points: (1) The hardships of a nomadic life necessitated occasionally the abandonment of the aged and the sick among various tribes of the North American Indians. (2) A person cured by some supernatural agency inaugurates a curing ceremony. (3) Women as well as men can conduct ceremonies.

SONGS OF THE MASKED DANCERS
(Apache)

1.

When the earth was made;
When the sky was made;
When my songs were first heard;
The holy mountain was standing toward me with life.

At the center of the sky, the holy boy walks four ways
with life.
Just mine, my mountain became; standing toward me
with life.
Gan [1] children became; standing toward me with life.

When the sun goes down to the earth,
Where Mescal Mountain lies with its head toward the
sunrise,
Black spruce became; standing up with me.

2.

Right at the center of the sky the holy boy with life
walks in four directions.
Lightning with life in four colors comes down four
times.
The place which is called black spot with life;
The place which is called blue spot with life;
The place which is called yellow spot with life;
The place which is called white spot with life;
They have heard about me,

[1] The Apache call their Masked Dancers "Gan."

The black Gans dance in four places.
The sun starts down toward the earth.

.3.

The living sky black-spotted;
The living sky blue-spotted;
The living sky yellow-spotted;
The living sky white-spotted;
The young spruce as girls stood up for their dance in
    the way of life.
When my songs first were, they made my songs with
    words of jet.
Earth when it was made,
Sky when it was made,
Earth to the end,
Sky to the end,
Black Gan, black thunder, when they came toward
    each other,
The various bad things that used to be vanished.
The bad wishes which were in the world vanished.
The lightning of black thunder struck four times for
    them.
It struck four times for me.

4.

When first my songs became,
When the sky was made,
When the earth was made,
The breath of the Gans on me made only of down;
When they heard about my life;
Where they got their life;

When they heard about me;
It stands.

5.

The day broke with slender rain.
The place which is called "lightning's water stands,"
The place which is called "where the dawn strikes,"
Four places where it is called "it dawns with life,"
I land there.
The sky boys, I go among them.
He came to me with long life.
When he talked over my body with the longest life,
The voice of thunder spoke well four times.
Holy sky boy spoke to me four times.
When he talked to me my breath became.

From Pliny Earle Goddard, *The Masked Dancers of the Apache*, p. 132 *et seq*. These songs are sung during the adolescence rites for girls. The Masked Dancers represent the gods. Symbolism of colors and numbers is highly developed with the Apache. See the following song.

SONG OF THE GOTAL CEREMONY
(MESCALERO APACHE)

The black turkey gobbler, under the east, the middle
of his trail; toward us it is about to dawn.
The black turkey gobbler, the tips of his beautiful tail;
above us the dawn whitens.
The black turkey gobbler, the tips of his beautiful
tail; above us the dawn becomes yellow.
The sunbeams stream forward, dawn boys, with
shimmering shoes of yellow.
On top of the sunbeams that stream toward us they
are dancing.
At the east the rainbow moves forward, dawn maidens,
with shimmering shoes and shirts of yellow dance
over us.
Beautifully over us it is dawning.

Above us among the mountains the herbs are
becoming green.
Above us on the top of the mountains the herbs are
becoming yellow.

Above us among the mountains, with shoes of yellow
I go around the fruits and the herbs that shimmer.
Above us among the mountains, the shimmering fruits
with shoes and shirts of yellow are bent toward
him.
On the beautiful mountains above it is daylight.

From P. E. Goddard, *Gotal: A Mescalero Apache Cere-
mony*, p. 392. This is the 53d. song of an adolescence rite

for girls; in the main, this ceremony is a dramatic represen-
tation of the creation and of the seasonal recreations of na-
ture. To *sing* of the day that dawns and of the things that
grow and mature will assure long life not only to the girl
that stands at the threshold of womanhood, but to all mem-
bers of the community.

SECTION FOUR:

From the Pueblos

SONG OF THE SKY LOOM
(TEWA)

O our Mother the Earth, O our Father the Sky,
Your children are we, and with tired backs
We bring you the gifts you love.
Then weave for us a garment of brightness;
May the warp be the white light of morning,
May the weft be the red light of evening,
May the fringes be the falling rain,
May the border be the standing rainbow.
Thus weave for us a garment of brightness,
That we may walk fittingly where birds sing,
That we may walk fittingly where grass is green,
O our Mother the Earth, O our Father the Sky.

From Herbert J. Spinden, *Songs of the Tewa*, p. 94. The
Tewa Indians belong to a group of Tanoan tribes inhabit-
ing the following pueblos: Nambé, San Ildefonso, San Juan,
Santa Clara, and Tesuque, all in New Mexico, and Hano
in northeastern Arizona. The sky loom, as Dr. Spinden
points out, refers to the small desert rain, so characteristic
of this part of the country: like wandering looms the rain-
showers hang from the sky. And the warp of the glittering
web seems like soft silver and the weft like amber or roseate
rays in the reflection of the late afternoon sun.

THAT MOUNTAIN FAR AWAY
(TEWA)

My home over there, my home over there,
My home over there, now I remember it!
And when I see that mountain far away,
Why, then I weep. Alas! what can I do?
What can I do? Alas! What can I do?
My home over there, now I remember it.

From *ibid.*, p. 72. "The Tewa Indian," says Dr. Spinden
in a note on page 114, "easily becomes homesick even when
distant a few miles from his native village."

THE WILLOWS BY THE WATERSIDE
(TEWA)

My little breath, under the willows by the waterside
    we used to sit,
And there the yellow cottonwood bird came and sang.
That I remember and therefore I weep.
Under the growing corn we used to sit,
And there the little leaf bird came and sang.
That I remember and therefore I weep.
There on the meadow of yellow flowers we used to
    walk.
Oh, my little breath! Oh, my little heart!
There on the meadow of blue flowers we used to walk.
Alas! how long ago that we two walked in that
    pleasant way.
Then everything was happy, but, alas! how long ago.
There on the meadow of crimson flowers we used to
    walk.
Oh, my little breath, now I go there alone in sorrow.

From *ibid.*, p. 73. Says Spinden in his interesting preface to this very valuable collection: "Love songs, except those which are supposed to have a magical and coercive quality of gaining affections and which might better be called love medicine, are not common among the tribes of the Great Plains. Nor are such songs listed by Ruth Bunzel among the kinds in use at Zuñi. The Tewa have them. . . . While these [love songs] are clearly enough of Indian composition, I believe the ultimate inspiration to have been Spanish." p. 35. The text given here is the close translation of a love song H. J. Spinden secured from the village of Santa Clara.

THE ORIGIN OF DEATH
(Cochiti)

They were coming up from Shipap. One of their children became sick and they did not know what was the trouble with him. They had never seen sickness before. They said to the Shkoyo [curing society] chief, "Perhaps our Mother in Shipap will help us. Go back and ask her to take away this trouble." He went back to our Mother and she said to him, "The child is dead. If your people did not die, the world would fill up and there would be no place for you to live. When you die, you will come back to Shipap to live with me. Keep on traveling and do not be troubled when your people die."

He returned to his people and told them what our Mother had said. In those days they treated one another as brothers, all the Indians of all the Pueblos. They planted corn with the digging stick and they were never tired; they dug trenches to irrigate their fields. The corn ripened in one day. When they came to Frijoles they separated, and the different pueblos went their own ways.

From Ruth Benedict, *Tales of the Cochiti Indians*, p. 5. The counsel of the Mother who resides at Shipap—the place of emergence and the realm of the dead—is quite in keeping with Pueblo philosophy. Excessive mourning is harmful and will interfere with the welfare not only of the living, but also of the dead. In another Cochiti story we hear that a child that had died could not find rest because her mother did not stop crying. Thus the chief priest of Shipap sent two messengers to the mother to let her know that "she should forget and not remember her daughter any more," for only then the child could go to the place where all Indians go—to Shipap. Pp. 131, 205.

SONG OF THE DEPARTING SPIRIT
(SANTO DOMINGO)

Part I

All the white-cloud eagles,
Lift me up with your wings and take me to Shipap.
And also you other eagles,
Come and lift me up with your wings, 'way up high,
    all over the world; no one can see the place where
    you are taking me.
'Way down in the southwest where our fathers and
    mothers have gone,
Put me there with your wings.

Part II

Thanks to Mother Earth, the whole world, and
    Mother Eagle.
Bless my people.
I am the spirit.
I am leaving for my own place where I shall be happy
    all my life.
I shall remember you people all the time.
I thank you all.

From Frances Densmore, *Music of Santo Domingo Pueblo
New Mexico*, pp. 67-8. After the burial has taken place,
"the medicine men shake their rattles first in a tremolo,
then in a steady beat as they sing this song. With Part I of
the song, two medicine men . . . go over to the people and
hold the eagle wings in front of the people as though lift-
ing the person and wafting him on his way. With Part II
they go back . . . to the sacred articles beside the altar,
and pray and give thanks."

SONG OF A CHILD'S SPIRIT
(SANTO DOMINGO)

I am on the way,
traveling the road to where the spirits live,
at Shipap.
I look at the road, far ahead, down that way.
Nothing happens to me, as I am a spirit.
I am a spirit, of course I am,
as I go on the nice clean road to Shipap.
It is true that my spirit meets the others
who come towards me.
I am glad to see them and be with them,
I have a right to be there.

I cannot help it; I must leave because the spirit
has called me back.
I must go, I must obey.
So I am going direct to my spirit.
There are places down there where all the people
live whom you have seen;
they have gone, when the time has come.

Now I cannot say what they will make of me.
I may take the form of a cloud;
I wish I could be a cloud.
I take the chance of whatever is offered to me.
When a cloud comes this way, you will say,
"That is he!"
When I get to the place of spirits,
I will hear everything you ask.
You must always remember me.

You have talked about me,
and in Shipap I can hear everything you say.

I am a spirit and I bless you.
I thank you for all you have done for me in past years.

I hope to see you some day.
We send you many good wishes, many good things.

Thank you.

From *ibid.*, p. 69.

A KATCINA SONG

(Zuñi)

In the west at Flower Mountain
A rain priest sits
His head feathered with cumulus clouds.
His words are of clouding over Itawana.
"Come let us arise now."
Thus along the shores of the encircling ocean
The rain makers say to one another.
Aha ehe
Aha ehe
In the south at Salt Lake Mountain
A rain priest sits
His head feathered with mist.
His words are of covering Itawana with rain.
"Come let us go."
Thus in all the springs
The rain makers say to one another.
Aha ehe
Aha ehe
"The beautiful world germinates.
The sun, the yellow dawn germinate."
Thus the corn plants say to one another.
They are covered with dew.
"The beautiful world germinates.
The sun, the yellow dawn germinate."
Thus the corn plants say to one another.
They bring forth their young.
Aha ehe
Aha ehe!

From Ruth L. Bunzel, *Zuñi Katcina: An Analytical Study*, p. 891. The Katcinas are supernaturals, identified with the dead and at the same time associated with clouds and rain. They are believed to live in a lake near Zuñi and to visit the village from time to time. They are impersonated in masks which the dancers wear during the Katcina ceremonies, the underlying idea of which is the desire to fertilize the earth and to call for the needed rain.—Itawana designates the realm of the dead.

PRAYER SPOKEN WHILE PRESENTING
AN INFANT TO THE SUN
(Zuñi)

Now this is the day.
Our child,
Into the daylight
You will go out standing.
Preparing for your day,
We have passed our days.
When all your days were at an end,
When eight days were past,
Our sun father
Went in to sit down at his sacred place.
And our night fathers,
Having come out standing to their sacred place,
Passing a blessed night.
Now this day,
Our fathers, Dawn priests,
Have come out standing to their sacred place,
Our sun father,
Having come out standing to his sacred place,
Our child, it is your day.
This day,
The flesh of the white corn, prayer meal,
To our sun father
This prayer meal we offer.

May your road be fulfilled.
Reaching to the road of your sun **father,**
When your road is fulfilled,
In your thoughts may we **live,**

May we be the ones whom your thoughts will
    embrace,
For this, on this day
To our sun father,
We offer prayer meal.
To this end:
May you help us all to finish our roads.

From Ruth L. Bunzel, *Zuñi Ritual Poetry*, p. 635. The
Zuñi child is born amid prayer and solemn ceremony.
Mathilde Stevenson describes in detail the beautiful cere-
mony of presenting the child to the cosmic power, the sun.
In her *"Religious Life of the Zuñi Child,"* p. 546, she
says: ". . . On the morning of the tenth day the child is
taken from its bed of sand, . . . and upon the left arm of
the paternal grandmother is carried for the first time into
the presence of the rising sun. To the breast of the child
the grandmother carrying it presses the ear of corn which
lay by its side during the ten days; to her left the mother
of the infant walks, carrying in her left hand the ear of
corn which lay at her side. Both women sprinkle a line of
sacred meal, emblematic of the straight road which the child
must follow to win the favor of its gods. Thus the first ob-
ject which the child is made to behold at the very dawn of
its existence is the sun, the great object of their worship,
and long ere the little lips can lisp a prayer it is repeated
for it by the grandmother."

THE GROWTH OF THE CORN

Prayer of the Fire Keeper at the Winter Solstice

(ZUÑI)

Yonder toward the east
With prayers
We made our road go forth.
How the world will be
How the days will be
We desired to know.
Perhaps if we are lucky
Our earth mother
Will wrap herself in a fourfold robe
Of white meal,
Full of frost flowers.
A floor of ice will spread over the world,
The forests.
The flesh of our earth mother
Will crack with cold.
Then in the spring when she is replete with
    living waters
All different kinds of corn
In our earth mother
We shall lay to rest.
With our earth mother's living waters
Into their sun father's daylight
They will come out standing;
Yonder to all directions
They will stretch out their hands calling
    for rain.

Then with their fresh waters
The rain makers will pass us on our roads.
Clasping their young ones in their arms
They will rear their children.
Gathering them into our houses,
With our thoughts following them,
Thus we shall always live.
That this may be
Eagerly we have awaited your day.

That yonder to where the life-giving road
    of your sun father comes
Your roads may reach;
That you may finish your roads;
For this I add to your breath.
To this end, my fathers,
My children,
May all of you be blessed with light.

From *ibid.,* pp. 640-2.

A WOMAN MOURNS FOR HER HUSBAND
(Zuñi)

. . . They came. They brought the ones who had been killed by the white people. My aunts were with me. My mother, my father, my aunts, held me and went with me. I came there; I was pregnant. They would not let me see him, my husband. Only my mother saw him. She told me. It was not good. . . . So they buried them in the graveyard, just before sunset.

. . . My grandfather took care of me. "It is very dangerous; you must fast. You must drink medicine. You must vomit. It is very dangerous. No one may touch you. It is very dangerous, you must fast. No one must touch you. You must stay alone. You must sit alone in the corner. Only your little boy may hold you. No one must touch you." Grandfather gathered medicine for me. This he soaked. He mixed it in a fine bowl. He brewed medicine. "This you will drink. You will vomit," he said to me. I was very wretched. This was very dangerous. When it was still early, when the sun had not yet risen, my grandfather took me far away. We scattered prayermeal. Here in the left hand I had black prayermeal, and here the right kind of prayermeal. When we had gone far I passed it four times over my head and scattered it. One should not speak. Again with this, I sprinkled prayermeal with a prayer:

My fathers,
Our Sun Father.

Our mother, Dawn,
Coming out standing to your sacred place,
Somewhere we shall pass you on your road.
This from which we form our flesh,
The white corn,
Prayermeal,
Shell,
Corn pollen,
I offer to you.
To the Sun who is our father,
To you I offer it
To you, I offer prayermeal.
To you, I offer corn pollen.
According to the words of my prayer,
So may it be.
May there be no deviation.
Sincerely from my heart I send forth my prayers.
To you, prayermeal, shell, I offer.
Corn pollen I offer.
According to the words of my prayer,
So may it be.

I would sprinkle prayermeal. I would inhale from the prayermeal. I would sprinkle the right kind of prayermeal. . . .

All alone I sat. I did not eat meat, nor salt, nor grease. I fasted from meat. It was very dangerous. Much my aunt, my grandfather exhorted me. When I was young, they said to me, "Fortunate you are to be alive. Sometimes you will be happy because of something. Sometimes you will be sorrowful. You will cry. This kind of person you shall be. You are fortunate to be alive." . . . And just so I have lived. . . . If one's husband dies one will not sleep. She will lie down as if she sleeps, and when sleep overcomes her she will sleep. But after a little while she will wake, and will not sleep. She will cry, she will be lonely. She will not care to eat. She will take thought of what to do and where to go. When a child or a relative dies, one cries for them properly. Husband and wife talk together to relieve their thoughts. Then they will forget their trouble. But when one's husband dies there is no happiness. . . .

It was very dangerous. It was the same as when an enemy dies, it was very dangerous. Four mornings I vomited. And so many days I sprinkled prayermeal far off, four times. And so many days I fasted. I was still a young woman . . .

For one year I would cry. I was thoughtful for my old husband. Then father spoke with me. Then I was happy. I did not worry. My uncle desired it for me. "It is all right, niece. Do not cry. It cannot be helped. It is ever thus. Do not think of where you have come from, but rather look forward to where you are to go . . ."

From Ruth Bunzel, *Zuñi Texts*, pp. 93-6.

PRAYER TO THE ANCIENTS AFTER HARVESTING
(ZuÑi)

From where you stay quietly,
Your little wind-blown clouds,
Your fine wisps of clouds,
Your massed clouds you will send forth
    to sit down with us;
With your fine rain caressing the earth,
With all your waters
You will pass to us on our roads.
With your great pile of waters,
With your fine rain caressing the earth,
You will pass to us on our roads.
My fathers,
Add to your hearts.
Your waters,
Your seeds,
Your long life,
Your old age
You will grant to us.
Therefore I have added to your hearts,
To the end, my fathers,
My children:
You will protect us.
All my ladder-descending children
Will finish their roads;
They will grow old.
You will bless us with life.

From Ruth Bunzel, *Zuñi Ritual Poetry*, pp. 622-3. Zuñi

prayers, says Ruth Bunzel, are highly formalized in content and mode of expression. Most of the prayers are requests accompanying offerings. "They have three sections, which always appear in the same order: A statement of the occasion, a description of the offering, and the request." The part from the Prayer to the Ancients brought here is the third one. The dead, the ancients, are believed to be the rain makers. They come back to the living in the rain clouds, bringing the blessing of life and fruitfulness. The offering of food to the dead forms an important part of the Zuñi household ritual. Before each meal a bit of food is scattered on the floor or thrown into the fire, accompanied by a short prayer. No child is weaned until he is able to make this offering by himself and utter his prayer to the ancients.

CREATION MYTH
(ZUÑI)

Before the beginning of the new-making, Awonawilona solely had being. There was nothing else whatsoever throughout the great spaces of the ages save everywhere black darkness in it, and everywhere void desolation.

In the beginning of the new-made, Awonawilona conceived within himself and thought outward in space, whereby mists of increase, steams potent of growth, were evolved and uplifted. Thus, by means of his innate knowledge, the All-Container made himself in person and form of the Sun, whom we hold to be our father and who thus came to exist and appear. With his appearance came the brightening of the spaces with light, and with the brightening of the spaces the great mist-clouds were thickened and fell, whereby evolved water in water; yea, and the world-holding sea. With his substance of flesh outdrawn from the surface of his person, the Sun Father formed the seed-stuff of twin-worlds impregnating therewith the great waters, and lo! in the heat of his light these waters of the sea grew green and scums grew upon them waxing wide and weighty until, behold! they became Awitelin Ts'ta, the "Fourfold-Containing Mother Earth," and Apoyan Tachu, the "All-Covering Father Sky." From the lying together of these twain upon the great world-waters, so vitalizing, terrestrial life was conceived; whence began all beings of earth, men and the creatures, in the Fourfold Womb of the Earth. Thereupon the Earth Mother repulsed the Sky Father, growing big and sinking deep into the embrace of the waters below, thus separating from the Sky Father in the embrace of the waters above. . . .

Now, like all the surpassing beings, the Earth Mother and the Sky Father were changeable, even as smoke in the wind; transmutable at thought, manifesting themselves in any form at will, like as dancers may by mask making . . . Thus as a man and a woman spake they, one to another:

"Behold," said the Earth Mother, as a great terraced bowl appeared at her hand and within it water, "this is as upon me the homes of my tiny children shall be. On the rim of each world country they wander in, terraced mountains shall stand, . . . whereby country shall be known from country, and within each, place from place. Behold again!" said she as she spat on the water, and rapidly smote and stirred it with her fingers. Foam formed, gathering about the terraced rim, mounting higher and higher. "Yea," she said, "and from my bosom they shall draw nourishment, for in such as this shall they find the substance of life whence we were ourselves sustained. For see!"

Then with her warm breath she blew across the terraces; white flecks of the foam broke away, and floating over above the water, were shattered by the cold breath of the Sky Father attending, and forthwith shed downward abundantly fine mist and spray! "Even so shall white clouds float up from the great waters at the borders of the world, and clustering about the mountain terraces of the horizons be borne aloft and abroad by the breaths of the surpassing soul beings, and of the children, and shall be hardened and broken by the cold, shedding downward, in rain spray,

241

the water of life, even in the hollow places of my lap. For therein shall chiefly nestle our children, mankind and creature-kind, for warmth in thy coldness! Even the trees on high mountains near the clouds . . . crouch low toward Mother Earth for warmth and protection.

"Even so!" said the Sky Father. "Yet not alone shalt thou be helpful unto our children, for behold!" and he spread his hand abroad with the palm downward and into all the wrinkles and crevices thereof he set the semblance of shining yellow corn grains; in the dark of the early world-dawn they gleamed like sparks of fire and moved as his hand was moved over the bowl, shining up from and also moving in the depth of the water therein.

From Frank Cushing, *Outlines of Zuñi Creation Myths*, pp. 379 ff. According to Benedict, Cushing's translation of the Zuñi myth of emergence is a "poeticized version that draws heavily upon his interpretative powers." Still, the philosophizings and schematic analogies of Cushing's tale "are characteristic of Zuñi esoteric speculative attempts at synthesis of ceremonies, clans, societies, directions of the compass, colors and patron animals." (p. 256). For a literal version of this myth compare the translation by Ruth Benedict in her brilliant study in *Zuñi Mythology*.

RAIN SONG
(Sia)

White floating clouds.
Clouds like the plains
Come and water the earth.
Sun, embrace the earth
That she may be fruitful.
Moon, lion of the north,
Bear of the west,
Badger of the south,
Wolf of the east,
Eagle of the heavens, shrew of the earth,
Elder war hero,
Warriors of the six mountains of the world,
Intercede with the cloud people for us,
That they may water the earth.
Medicine bowl, cloud bowl, and water vase,
Give us your hearts,
That the earth may be watered.
I make the ancient road of meal,
That my song may straight pass over it—the ancient
    road.
White shell bead woman,
Who lives where the sun goes down,
Mother whirlwind, mother Sûs'sistumako,
Mother Ya-ya, creator of good thoughts,
Yellow woman of the north, blue woman of the west,
Red woman of the south, white woman of the east,
Slightly yellow woman of the zenith,
And dark woman of the nadir,
I ask your intercession with the cloud people.

From Mathilde Stevenson, *The Sia*, p. 130.

THE RETURN TO THE OLD GODS
(Hopi)

My earliest memories of my real grandfather, Ho-mikniwa, are full of kind feelings. I slept with him much of the time. In the morning before sunrise he sang to me and told me stories. He took me to his fields, where I helped him to work or slept under a peach tree. Whenever he saw me make a circle he stepped cautiously around it, saying that he had to watch me lest I block his path with my antelope power. He kept reminding me of this power. He also took me through the fields to collect healing herbs. I watched him sprinkle corn meal and pray to the Sun God before picking up leaves or berries or digging medicine roots. Whenever mothers brought their sick children to our house, I watched him take their pinches of meal, step outside, pray, and sprinkle them to the Sun God, Moon, or the stars, and to his special medicine god. Then he would return to the patient, blow upon his hands, and begin his treatment. He was respected by all. Even Mr. Voth, the missionary, came to him to learn about plants and herbs. He taught the white man many things. He also taught me almost all I ever learned about plants. He advised me to keep bad thoughts out of my mind, to face the east, look to the bright side of life, and learn to show a shining face even when unhappy.

Mr. Voth and the Christians came to Oraibi and preached Jesus in the plaza where the Katcinas danced. The old people paid no attention, but we children were told to receive any gifts and clothing. Mr. Voth never preached Christ to me alone but talked to us in groups. He said that Jesus Christ was our Saviour and suffered for our sins. He told us that Jesus was a good shepherd and that we were sheep or goats. We were to ask Jesus for whatever we wanted. Oranges and candy looked pretty good to me so I prayed for them. I said, "Jesus, give me some oranges and candy." Then I looked up into the sky, but I never saw him throw down anything to me. Mr. Voth claimed that our gods were not good but the old people pointed out to us that when the Katcinas danced in the Plaza, it often rained. Even as a child I was taught that the missionaries had no business condemning our gods and that it might cause droughts and famine.

One winter morning in February I saw a tall, strange Katcina coming into the village, blowing a bone whistle and uttering a long-drawn "Hu-hu-huhuhu." When he entered the Plaza women and children threw pinches of corn meal upon him and took sprigs of green corn and of spruce boughs from his tray. Two other Katcinas joined him near the kiva, where they were holding a ceremony, blew tobacco smoke on the backs of the Katcinas, and sprinkled them with corn meal. A number of different Katcinas, some running crosslegged, came through the streets handing out gifts. Some of us received bows, arrows, rattles, and Katcina dolls. Other Katcinas came into the village bringing bean sprouts in their baskets. We were in the Plaza watching them. Suddenly my mother threw a blanket over my head. When she uncovered me the Katcinas were all gone and the people were looking up in the sky and watching them fly about—they said. I looked up but could see nothing. My mother laughed and said that I must be blind.

I later saw some giantlike Katcinas stalking into the village with long black bills and big sawlike teeth. One carried a rope to lasso disobedient children. He stopped at a certain house and called for a boy. "You have been naughty," he scolded. "You fight with other children. You kill chickens. You pay no attention to the old people. We have come to get you and eat you." The boy cried and promised to behave better. The giants became angrier and threatened to tie him up and take him away. But the boy's parents begged for his life and offered fresh meat in his place. The giant reached out his hand as if to grab the boy but took the meat instead. Placing it in his basket, he warned the boy that he would get just one chance to change his conduct. I was frightened and got out of sight. I heard that sometimes these giants captured boys and really ate them.

By the time I was six . . . I had learned to find my way about the mesa and to avoid graves, shrines, and harmful plants, to size up people, and to watch out for witches. I was above average height and in good health. My hair was clipped just above the eyes, but left long in back and tied in a knot at the nape of my neck. I had almost lost an eye. I wore silver earrings, a missionary shirt or one made of a flour sack, and was always bare-legged, except for a blanket in cold weather. When no whites were present, I went naked. I slept out on the housetop in summer and sometimes in the kiva with other boys in winter. I could help plant and weed, went out herding with my father, and was a kiva trader. I owned a dog and a cat, a small bow made by my father, and a few good arrows. Sometimes I carried stolen matches tucked in the hem of my shirt collar. I could ride a tame burro, kill a kangaroo rat, and catch small birds, but I could not make fire with a drill and I was not a good runner like the other fellows. But I had made a name for myself by healing people; and I had almost stopped running after my mother for her milk.

[Don had been sent to a white man's school, and the results of this education after the first year he is summing up in this way:]

On June the fourteenth my father came for me and we returned home, riding burros and bringing presents of calico, lamps, shovels, axes, and other tools. It was a joy to get home again, to see all my folks, and to tell about my experiences at school. I had learned many English words and could recite part of the Ten Commandments. I knew how to sleep on a bed, pray to Jesus, comb my hair, eat with a knife and fork, and use a toilet. I had learned that the world is round instead of flat, that it is indecent to go naked in the presence of girls. I had also learned that a person thinks with his head instead of his heart.

[At the conclusion of the last year of the time he had spent in schools, and before his return to Hopiland, Don expresses his feelings about the past and his future in these words:]

As I lay on my blanket I thought about my schooldays and all that I had learned. I could talk like a gentleman, read, write, and cipher. I could name all the states in the Union with their capitals, repeat the names of all the books in the Bible, quote a hundred verses of Scripture, sing more than two dozens of Christian hymns and patriotic songs, debate, shout football yells, swing my partners in square dances, bake bread, sew well enough to make a pair of trousers, and tell dirty Dutchman stories by the hour. It was important that I had learned how to get along with white men and earn money by helping them. But my death experience had taught me that I had a Hopi Spirit Guide whom I must follow if I wished to live. I wanted to become a real Hopi again, to sing the good old Katcina songs, and to feel free to make love without fear of sin or a rawhide.

I had learned a great lesson and now knew that the ceremonies handed down by our fathers mean life and security, both now and hereafter. I regretted that I had ever joined the Y.M.C.A. and decided to set myself against Christianity once and for all. I could see that the old people were right when they insisted that Jesus Christ might do for modern whites in a good climate, but that the Hopi gods had brought success to us in the desert ever since the world begun.

With marriage I began a life of toil and discovered that education had spoiled me for making a living in the desert. I was not hardened to heavy work in the heat and dust, and I did not know how to get rain, control winds, or even predict good and bad weather, I could not grow young plants in dry, wind-beaten, and worm-infested sand drifts; nor could I shepherd a flock of sheep through storm, drought, and disease. . . .

"Talayesva," my uncles and fathers said, "you must stay home and work hard like the rest of us. Modern ways help a little; but the whites come and go, while we Hopi stay on forever. Corn is our mother—and only the Cloud People can send rain to make it grow. . . . They come from the six directions to examine our hearts. If they are good they gather above us in cotton masks and white robes and drop rain to quench our thirst and nourish our plants. . . . Keep bad thoughts behind you and face the rising sun with a cheerful spirit, as did our ancestors in the days of plenty. Then rain fell on all the land." . . .

I thought I would be willing to go back to the very beginning of Hopi life, wear native clothes, and hunt wild deer. I let my hair grow long, tied it in a knot at the nape of my neck, and stored my citizen's clothes in a gunnysack. I ate old Hopi foods, practiced the Katcina and Wowochim songs, and brought sand up the mesa in my blanket to start a bean crop in the kiva.

I joined herds with . . . three old men—and had to go out and herd in the worst weather—in sleet, snow, and rain when it was too cold to ride a horse, and when shepherd and flock had to run to keep warm. Strong winds drove sand into my face and eyes, filled my ears and nose, and made it difficult to eat my lunch without catching mouthfuls of grit. My clothes were often heavy with sand and chafed me as I walked. . . . Dust and snowstorms scattered my flock and forced me to search days for stray animals. . . . Storms frequently caught sheep in labor or drove them from newborn lambs. These young things were beaten about and often killed by hail, water, and wind. I would gather

249

wet, shivering lambs in my arms and bury them up to their eyes in warm, dry sand from a sheltered bank. I studied clouds and paid close attention to my dreams in order to escape being trapped by storms too far from shelter.

In July I was happy to bring a few sweet-corn stalks into the village for the Niman Dance. I made dolls and tied them to cattail stems while my mother prepared little plaques three inches across. We took these things up on the roof and presented them to the hawks on the day of Niman. We feasted and danced all day and presented sweet corn, dolls, and other gifts to the children. The Katcinas were sent away at sunset with urgent prayers for rain upon our drooping crops. Nearly every man broke off a spruce bough to plant in his cornfield. Next morning we choked the hawks to send them home, plucked their feathers, tied *pahos* to their necks, wings, and feet, took them out in the direction whence they came, and buried them with corn meal. We told them to hasten home and send us rain. I then took a spruce bough to my cornfield, set it in the sand, held meal in my right hand, and prayed silently to the sun, moon, and stars for a good crop. I also sprinkled a path of corn meal and wished for rain, taking care not to step on the meal. When it did rain, the ceremonial officer said that it was proof that our prayers had reached the Six Point Cloud People.

The land was very dry, the crops suffered, and even the Snake Dance failed to bring much rain. We tried to discover the reason for our plight, and remembered the Rev. Voth who had stolen so many of our ceremonial secrets and had even carried off sacred images and altars to equip a museum and become a rich man. When he had worked here in my boyhood, the Hopi were afraid of him and dared not lay their hands on him or any other missionary, lest they be jailed by the whites. During the ceremonies this wicked man would force his way into the kiva and write down everything he saw. He wore shoes with solid heels, and when the Hopis tried to put him out of the kiva he would kick them. He came back to Oraibi on a visit and took down many more names. Now I was grown, educated in the whites' school, and had no fear of this man. When I heard that he was in my mother's house I went over and told him to get out. I said: "You break the commandments of your own God. He has ordered you never to steal or to have any other Gods before him. He has told you to avoid all graven images; but you have stolen ours, and set them up in your museum. This makes you a thief and an idolator who can never go to heaven." I knew the Hopi Cloud People despised this man, and even though he was now old and wore a long beard I had a strong desire to seize him by the collar and kick him off the mesa.

One day I visited Kalnimptewa, my father's old blind brother, and said: "Father, as I stood in my door I saw a Hopi missionary preaching to you from a Bible." "Yes," the old man answered, "he talked a great deal, but his words failed to touch me. He warned me that it would not be long before Jesus Christ would come down from the sky, say a few sharp words, and destroy all disbelievers. He said that my only chance to escape destruction was to confess and pray to his holy God. He urged me to hurry before it was too late, for a great flood was coming to Oraibi. I told him that I had prayed for rain all my life and nobody expected a flood in Oraibi. I also said that I was an old man and would not live very long, so he could not frighten me that way. . . ." He concluded: "Now, Talayesva, my son, you are a full-grown man, a herder and a farmer who supports a family, and such work means a happy life. When our ceremonies come round, pray faithfully to our Gods, and increase the good life of your family, and in this way you will stay happy." I thanked him and went home feeling confident that I would never pay any serious attention to the Christians. Other Gods may help some people, but my only chance for a good life is with the Gods of my fathers. I will never forsake them, even though their ceremonies die out before my eyes and all their shrines are neglected.

Selected from Leo W. Simmons, *Sun Chief, the Autobiography of a Hopi Indian*. Don's autobiography, as edited by Dr. Simmons, is, though a trifle self-conscious, undoubtedly a major contribution to the science of culture contact. The *Leitmotif* throughout is the problem of how a not quite average personality reacts who stands between two utterly different cultures, accepted wholly by neither. To shape a livable present out of a crumbling past and a threatening future is the motivating power that determines most of Don's activities, cravings, and militant attitudes.

In this connection it is of psychological interest to learn that the investigator who spends some time in the midst of the "peaceful people" is struck with the many cases of maladjustment within and without. Dorothy Eggan in her paper "The General Problem of Hopi Adjustment" *(American Anthropologist,* vol. 45, 1943, pp. 357-373) traces three formative pressures that were necessarily to build up an attitude of permanent anxiety and ambivalent emotions. The first pressure she sees in the Hopi culture pattern itself (early inculcation of fear and oversharp restriction of all forms of aggression); the second in the environment that makes the struggle for existence a source of constant fear; but Hopi character of today is mainly the result of the devastating contact with the whites, it is the tragic outcome of "frustrating acculturation influences." Dr. Kluckhohn's paper on "The Personal Document in Anthropological Science," 1945, presents a helpful guide in the study of "primitive" personality.

SECTION FIVE:

From California

A PAIUTE AUTOBIOGRAPHY
(Eastern California)

I learned to hunt when I was just a young boy. I made all my own bows and arrows and hunted in the valley for rabbits and ducks. I picked up this knowledge partly from the boys who always know something about it, and partly from my father's teachings.

Once, while my people were visiting my father's village (he was born in his mother's village), my father told me about hunting. He said to me: "You go up toward Black Mountain. Whatever comes near you, will come from the north. It will be a mountain sheep. You will shoot it and then you will follow it southward. You will get it." *Later I had a dream* and saw the thing my father had told me about. I was standing in the mountains, watching some mountain sheep come toward me. When they were close I took two arrows and shot, but missed. "That is strange," I said, "after what my father told me. What he said must be untrue." A few years later the dream came again, and I knew that my father was wrong. I said to myself: "What my father told me is false. After this, when I am hunting, I will use my own judgment." After that I relied upon myself and became a very successful hunter.

When I was still a young man, I saw Birch Mountain in a dream. It said to me: "You will always be strong and well. Nothing can hurt you, and you will live to an old age." After this Birch Mountain came and spoke to me whenever I was in trouble and told me that I would be all right. That is why nothing has happened to me and why I am so old now.

Not long after this, when I was bewitched, my power helped me out. . . . The witch doctor came to a bad end like all people who do evil things.

I also was interested in women. My soul confessed it. It once said to me in a dream: "One thing I cannot get away from is love for women. I can get along without other things, but I cannot get along without women. I shall never be able to outlive this." I found that this was true and spent much time in the company of women.

But it soon brought me trouble, and I had to call upon my power. . . . I became so sick that I gave myself up for dead. My soul admitted that I would have to die.

I died and my soul started southward, toward *tüpüsi witü*. While I was traveling, I looked down [apparently the journey was through the air], and my soul saw a stick in the ground not quite as tall as a man. . . . I turned to the stick and said: "This is the soul stick." I seized the stick and looked back toward my mountain, which was my power. I knew then that I would be all right and live forever, for whenever a soul going south sees the soul stick, it knows that it will come back. . . . My power from Birch Mountain helped me just as much in hunting as in sickness. . . .

I was a young man when I promised myself to be a peaceful person. My soul said to me in a dream: "I shall never kill anyone; but in self-defense I will fight it out to the finish." . . .

Whenever I dream, especially when it is a bad

dream which means trouble, I talk to something in the darkness. I talk to my power. That is why I have lived so long. If I had not called upon my power, accident or disaster would have overtaken me long ago. Even when I have sex dreams, I talk to the night, because if I should not pay attention to them, they would continue and lead to fits. . . .

When I die, my soul will go south to the land of the dead. It will stay there by the ocean, and I will have nothing to do but enjoy myself.

From Julian H. Steward, *Two Paiute Autobiographies,* pp. 423-38. As the Paiutes are neighbors of the Havasupai, the analyses Leslie Spier provides of the dream experiences of the latter are valid also for the Paiutes. Says Spier in his work on the Havasupai, p. 333: "A distinction is drawn between unimportant and significant dreams. While there are no definite criteria to distinguish them, it seems that those in which the dead, ghosts, or spirits figure are generally held significant. The real test seems to be the subsequent occurrence of an important happening, whereupon the appropriate dream is assigned as a forecast of the event." In this connection there may be quoted one of Spier's informants: "I have dreamed that I was hunting and got some deer, but when I tried next morning I failed. I dreamed falsely: one does not have to dream the truth." And again the same informant: "It is bad to dream of the dead. I do not want to dream of them . . . [but when I have dreamt of them] I blow into my hands and brush them down my face and body. So I brush the dream away into the night." Perfect self-therapy!

This specimen found a place in this collection not because of any outstanding literary significance either in form or content, but because it tells in a pleasingly direct way of a culture trait, common to most of the Californian and southwestern desert tribes: the dream. It is the dream of the individual that directs and dominates his life to the exclusion of any interference from group, organized priesthood, or tradition, though, of course, the dreams run along certain channels, grooved out by tradition and the general narrow scope of the various Californian culture groups.

COYOTE AND DEATH
(Wintu)

A long time ago, when the first people lived, all of them came together and decided to build a staircase to heaven. They set to work. Buzzard was their leader. He said, "When people are old and blind they will go to heaven and become young and healthy again. There will be a camping place there with plenty of wood and a spring."

Coyote came along. They were working. Coyote said, "Nephews, what are you doing?" They paid no attention to him. Then he said, "Get in the shade and rest. It is too hot to work." So finally they did. They told Coyote what they were doing. Coyote said, "It would be a good idea to have people die. People can go to burials and cry. It would be nice."

"Your idea is not good," they said.

Coyote argued in favor of death. Then Buzzard and the others said, "When acorns ripen they will have no shells. Snow will be salmon flour."

Coyote was against this too. He said, "Acorns should have shells so that the boys and girls can shell them and throw them at each other in the evening and have a good time. Snow should be cold, and when people go out to hunt in it they will die. That is the way it will be good."

Finally all the people became very angry and destroyed their work.

From DuBois and Demetracopoulou, *Wintu Myths*, p. 299.

SONG OF THE SPIRIT

(Luiseño)

At the time of death,
When I found there was to be death,
I was very much surprised.
All was failing.
My home,
I was sad to leave it.

I have been looking far,
Sending my spirit north, south, east,
    and west,
Trying to escape from death,
But could find nothing,
No way of escape.

From Constance G. DuBois, *The Religion of the Luiseño Indians*, p. 110. (Part of the Quiot story.) The Eagle, it is said, tried to escape from death. He went to all the corners of the earth to escape—he also went to Temecula; there he heard a spirit singing, from far away, telling him that it was no use trying to escape—death would come to everybody.

THE CREATION MYTH

(Luiseño)

In the beginning all was empty space. Ké-vish-a-tak-vish was the only being. This period was called *Om-ai-ya-mai,* signifying emptiness, nobody there. Then came the time called *Ha-ruh-rug,* upheaval, things coming into shape. Then a time called *Chu-tu-tai,* the falling of things downward, and after this, *Yu-vai-to-vai,* things working in darkness without the light of sun or moon. Then came the period *Tul-mul Pu-shim,* signifying that deep down in the heart of the earth things were working together.

Then came *Why-yai Pee-vai,* a gray glimmering like the whiteness of hoar frost; and then, *Mit'ai Kwai-rai,* the dimness of twilight. Then came a period of cessation, *Na-kai Ho-wai-yai,* meaning things at a standstill. Then Ké-vish-a-tak-vish made a man, Tuk-mit, the Sky, and a woman, To-mai-yo-vit, the Earth. There was no light, but in the darkness these two became conscious of each other.

"Who are you," asked the man.

"I am To-mai-yo-vit. I am stretched, I am extended. I shake, I resound. I am diminished, I am earthquake. I revolve, I roll, I disappear. And who are you?"

"I am Ké-vish-a-tak-vish. I am night. I am inverted. I cover, I rise. I devour, I drain [by death]. I seize, I send away the souls of men. I cut, I sever life."

"Then you are my brother."

"Then you are my sister."

263

And by her brother, the Sky, the Earth conceived and became the mother of all things.

From Constance G. DuBois, "Mythology of the Mission Indians," *Journal of American Folklore,* Vol. 19. See also A. L. Kroeber, *Handbook of the Indians of California,* p. 677.

CURING SONG
(YUMA)

Your heart is good.
[The Spirit] Shining Darkness will be here.
You think only of sad unpleasant things,
You are to think of goodness.
Lie down and sleep here.
Shining darkness will join us.
You think of this goodness in your dream.
Goodness will be given to you,
I will speak for it, and it will come to pass.
It will happen here,
I will ask for your good,
It will happen as I sit by you,
It will be done as I sit here in this place.

From C. Daryll Forde, *Ethnography of the Yuma Indians*, p. 190.

A MEDICINE MAN TELLS OF HIS
CURING POWER
(Yuma)

I had my dreams first when I was quite young, but I did not try to cure until I was an old man. I remembered them quite clearly always and never forgot anything in them.

If I hear of a sick person something tells me whether his illness is one I would be good for. This may happen even if I have not had a dream and power especially for his sickness. If I feel right I know I will be able to cure the man. When I have a good feeling I am very strong and light inside. . . . The patient and the relations know too, for I seem to draw the sick man to me. When I am called to go to the sick man I have a special feeling, it is like being back on the mountain. There is some fluid in me which I have drawn from the air, and I do not mind walking a great distance. I do not know how far I have traveled. When I work on the patient it does not tire me at all and it makes me very happy.

Sometimes I feel quite different about it, I don't get any good feeling and though I do my best I do not often cure then. I don't get any feeling of lightness, and when I go away from the sick man I don't want to return to him. I feel heavy and tired and very sleepy that night. I think about all the jobs I have to do around here and cannot keep my mind on the sick man. I know it is really no good me trying to help him, even if I have had a dream for his sickness."

From *ibid.,* p. 184. Told by Manuel Thomas.

THE CREATOR, THE SNAKE, AND
THE RABBIT

From the Creation Tale

(MARICOPA)

After Cipas arranged that people should die, he said, "Even after they die, they should have life again." And he said that even after his death, he would have a spirit life.

Then he sat down to wait for all his people to talk. The Mission Indians were the first to talk. The Maricopa talked next. Then all the tribes spoke in turn. The Chemehuevi talked in the middle of the night, so their language is unintelligible to anybody else. All the tribes here had spoken. The white people were the very last to speak. It was said, that like a younger child, they were cry-babies. So the Creator did everything to soothe them, hence they are richer than any of the Indians. . . .

When everybody could speak, that is including rabbits and all other kinds of animals, he built a big house for them. This held all the beings he had created. When morning came they would all go out to play together; all the games of which they could think. Toward evening they would all go into the house. Then he also made a snake. It had no teeth. It was gentle. Its name was Kinyamás Kasur, meaning fragile and limp. They would take the snake and hit each other with it. The rabbit always got the snake and played with it. He would bring it out, so that they could play, hitting each other with it until it was half dead. . . .

[Once] early in the morning they all went out to play. The Creator was lying right by the door. The snake crawled up to him. The Creator asked him what he wanted. The snake said that he only crawled up because of his poor condition; he was not being treated right. He had life just like the others: he did not see why he was roughly treated by everyone in that house. The Creator told him to sit there and wait for the sun to rise. Then the Creator took some coals and chewed them into tiny bits. They both sat there; the snake facing the east as the sun rose. Then the Creator told him to open his mouth. This he did. Then the Creator put the coal and the sun rays together in it for teeth. The snake now had teeth, so he went back able to protect himself.

Toward evening when everybody returned to the house, they sent the rabbit again to get the snake. As she [sic] reached for the snake, she was bitten. She suffered with pain for just a short time and died at midnight. . . .

After the rabbit died they felt bad over their great loss. So instead of going out to play, they remained quiet mourning their sister. Then they began to wonder who had put teeth in the snake's mouth. They discovered who it was: their father, who had taken pity on the poor snake. Then they wondered why he did not feel sorry for the rabbit. Then they said they would kill their father, if only someone knew how. They thought he, too, ought to die.

Bullfrog was the one who knew how to do it. The frog sank into the ground and went under a slough where the old man used to swim. If he went swimming again, the frog was to drink up all the water in the slough. He did this. As soon as the old man got out, he felt sick as he was going home.

[He tries to recover by lying in four places and by eating four remedies, but nothing helps.]

He said: "All these things I have tried in order to recover from my sickness, but they do no good. I have not been with you long enough to tell you all I know. Sickness must come to people just as it did to me." ... Then he died on the fourth day.

When Cipas died he went under the earth. He lies there yet. Whenever he yawns a little and turns over, an earthquake is caused.

From Leslie Spier, *Yuman Tribes of the Gila River*, pp. 347-50 (condensed).

WHY HUMANS SING FOR THEIR SICK
AND THEIR DEAD
(MARICOPA)

[Coyote, in thwarting repeatedly the efforts of the transformers, has gotten into serious trouble. He would have died had not Namet Hatagult, one of the transformers, taken pity on him.]

Namet Hatagult said: "Poor brother, I shall sing a song for you [i.e. cure you]." At the first song, Coyote could barely open his eyes. At the second song, he moved his feet just a little. At the third song, he began to keep time with the singing: *pat, pat.* Then, at the fourth song, he rose and danced around: *stamp, stamp.* Because of this, the Mohave still continue to sing for their sick and dead.

When Namet found the other [transformer] had stayed so long, he came down to see what was happening. When he reached the ground, he said: "If I had stayed away from my sick brother altogether, humans might do the same. A family may have disputes, but because of sickness they should forgive one another. For this reason, I will forgive my brother, who has done me great wrong."

From *ibid.,* p. 359.

A PRAYER

(Yokuts, California)

Do you see me!
See me, Tüüshiut!
See me, Pamashiut!
See me, Yuhahait!
See me, Eshepat!
See me, Pitsuriut!
See me, Tsuksit!
See me, Ukat!

Do you all help me!
My words are tied in one
With the great mountains,
With the great rocks,
With the great trees,
In one with my body
And my heart.
Do you all help me
With supernatural power
And you, day,
And you, night!
All of you see me
One with this world.

From A. L. Kroeber, *Handbook of the Indians of California*, p. 511.

GUDATRIGAKWITL AND THE CREATION
(Wishosk)

At first there were no trees nor rivers and no people on the earth. Nothing except ground was visible. There was no ocean. Then Gudatrigakwitl was sorry that it was so. He thought, "How is it that there are no animals?" He looked, but he saw nothing. Then he deliberated. He thought, "I will try. Somebody will live on the earth. But what will he use?" Then he decided to make a boat for him. He made things by joining his hands and spreading them. He used no tools. In this way he made people. The first man was *wat,* the abalone. The first people were not right. They all died. Gudatrigakwitl thought that they were bad. He wanted good people who would have children. At first he wanted every man to have ten lives. When he was an old man he was to become a boy again. Afterwards Gudatrigakwitl found that he could not do this. He gave the people all the game, the fish, and the trees. . . .

Gudatrigakwitl used no sand or earth or sticks to make the people; he merely thought and they existed.

Gudatrigakwitl thought: "When something is alive, like a plant, it will not die. It will come up again from the roots and grow again and again. So it will be with men, and animals, and everything alive. . . ."

Gudatrigakwitl left the people all kinds of dances. He said: "When there is a festivity, call me. If some do not like what I say, let them be. But those to whom I leave my instructions, who will teach them to their children, will be well. Whenever you are badly off, call me. I can save you in some way, no matter how great the difficulty. If a man does not call me, I will let him go. . . ."

Gudatrigakwitl went all over the world looking. Then he made everything. When he had finished everything he made people.

Gudatrigakwitl is not called on every day. He is called only when a man is in difficulty.

From A. L. Kroeber, "Wishosk Myths," *Journal of American Folklore*, Vol. 18.

SECTION SIX:

From the Northwest

MEDICINE FORMULA

(TAKELMA, OREGON)

[When the new moon appears it is shouted to:]

I shall prosper,
I shall yet remain alive.
Even if people do say of me,
"Would that he died!"
Just like thee shall I do,
Again shall I arise.
Even if all sorts of evil beings devour thee,
When frogs eat thee up,
Many evil beings—lizards,
Even when those eat thee up,
Still dost thou rise again.
Just like you will I do in time to come.
Bo!

From Edward Sapir, *Takelma Texts*, p. 197.

LOVE SONG

(NOOTKA)

No matter how hard I try
to forget you,
you always
come back to my mind,
and when you hear me singing
you may know
I am weeping for you.

From Frances Densmore, *Nootka and Quileute Music,*
p. 327.

SONG TO BRING FAIR WEATHER
(Nootka)

You, whose day it is, make it beautiful.
Get out your rainbow colors,
So it will be beautiful.

PLAINT AGAINST THE FOG
(Nootka)

Don't you ever,
You up in the sky,
Don't you ever get tired
Of having the clouds between you and us?

From *ibid.*, p. 285, p. 284.

LOVE SONG OF THE DEAD

Heard on Shell-Island

(KWAKIUTL)

You are hard-hearted against me, my dear,
ha ha ye ya ha ha!
You are cruel against me, my dear,
ha ha ye ya ha ha!
For I am tired waiting for you to come here, my dear,
ha ha ye ya ha ha!
Now I shall cry differently on your account, my dear,
ha ha ye ya ha ha!
Ah, I shall go down to the lower world, there I shall
cry for you, my dear,
ha ha ye ya ha ha!

From Franz Boas, *The Ethnology of the Kwakiutl*, p. 1306.

PRAYER TO THE YOUNG CEDAR
(KWAKIUTL)

The woman goes into the woods to look for young cedar trees. As soon as she finds them, she picks out one that has no twists in the bark, and whose bark is not thick. She takes her hand adze and stands under the young cedar tree, and looking upward to it, she prays, saying:

Look at me, friend!
I come to ask for your dress,
For you have come to take pity on us;
For there is nothing for which you cannot be
    used, . . .
For you are really willing to give us your dress,
I come to beg you for this,
Long-Life maker,
For I am going to make a basket for lily roots
    out of you.
I pray you, friend, not to feel angry
On account of what I am going to do to you;
And I beg you, friend, to tell our friends about
    what I ask of you.
Take care, friend!
Keep sickness away from me,
So that I may not be killed by sickness or in war,
    O friend!

This is the prayer that is used by those who peel cedar bark of young cedar trees and of old cedar trees.

From *ibid.*, p. 619.

PARTING SONG

Sung by Ts'esquane on His Deathbed
(Kwakiutl)

Farewell, O friends! for I am leaving you, O friends!
a ye ha a, a ye ya ha, aye!
O friends! do not take it too much to heart that I am
leaving you, O friends! *a ye ya ha a* . . .
O brothers! do not take it too much to heart that I am
leaving you, O friends, *a ye ya ha a* . . .
O sisters! do not feel sorrowful because I am leaving
you, O sisters, *a ye ya ha* . . .
I was told by the one who takes care of me that I shall
not stay away long, that I shall come back to you,
O friends! *a ye ya ha* . . .
I mean, O friends! that you shall not feel too sorrowful
when I leave you, O friends! *a ye ya ha a, a ye ya
ha, aye a!*

From *ibid.*, p. 1307. A few lines of repetition omitted.

PRAYER OF A MAN WHO FOUND A DEAD KILLER WHALE

(KWAKIUTL)

"Oh, it is great how you lie there on the ground,
Great Supernatural One.
What has made you unlucky?
Why, great and good one, are you lying here on the
    ground?
Friend, Supernatural One,
Why have you been unlucky, friend, for I thought you
could never be overcome, by all the Short-Life-Maker
    Women.
Now, you great and good one, have you been
    overcome
by the one who does as he pleases to us, friend.
I mean this, that you may wish that I shall inherit
your quality of obtaining easily all kinds of game
and all kinds of fish,
you Great Supernatural One, friend,
you Long-Life Maker.
And also that you protect me,
that I may not have any trouble, Supernatural One,
And also that it may not penetrate me,
the evil word of those who hate me among my fellow
    men,
And that only may penetrate themselves
the curses of those who wish me to die quickly.
I mean this, friend,
Only have mercy on me

283

that nothing evil may befall me,
Great Supernatural One," says he.
"*Wâ,* I will do this," says the man
on behalf of the one he found dead.

From Franz Boas, *The Religion of the Kwakiutl In-dians,* Vol. 2, p. 184.

PRAYER OF A MOTHER WHOSE CHILD DIED

(KWAKIUTL)

When it is the first-born child of the one who has just for the first time given birth, a young woman, then the woman is really fond of her child. Then she engages a carver to make a little canoe and all kinds of playthings for the boy. And if it is a girl, then she engages a doll maker to make dolls of alder wood, and women are hired by her to make little mats and little dishes and little spoons. Then her child begins to get sick, and not long is sick the child when it dies and the woman carries in her arms her child. Then all the relatives of the woman come to see her and all the women wail together. As soon as all the women stop crying the mother of the child speaks aloud. She says:

"Ah, ah, ah! What is the reason, child, that you have done this to me? I have tried hard to treat you well when you came to me to have me for your mother. Look at all your toys. What is the reason that you desert me, child? May it be that I did something, child, to you in the way I treated you, child? I will try better when you come back to me, child. Please, only become at once well in the place to which you are going. As soon as you are made well, please, come back to me, child. Please, do not stay away there. Please, only have mercy on me who is your mother, child," says she.

Then they put the child in the coffin, and they put it up on a hemlock tree. That is the end.

From Franz Boas, *ibid.*, p. 202.

285

THE IMAGE THAT CAME TO LIFE
(TLINGIT)

A young chief on the Queen Charlotte Islands married, and soon afterwards his wife fell ill. Then he sent around everywhere for the very best shamans. If there was a very fine shaman at a certain village, he would send a canoe there to bring him. None of them could help her, however, and after she had been sick for a very long time she died.

Now the young chief felt very badly over the loss of his wife. He went from place to place after the best carvers in order to have them carve an image of his wife, but no one could make anything to look like her. All this time there was a carver in his own village who could carve much better than all the others. This man met him one day and said, "You are going from village to village to have wood carved like your wife's face, and you cannot find anyone to do it, can you? I have seen your wife a great deal walking with you. . . . I am going to try to carve her image if you will allow me."

Then the carver went after a piece of red cedar and began working upon it. When he was through, he went to the young chief and said, "Now you can come along and look at it." So the chief went with him, and, when he got inside, he saw his dead wife sitting there just as she used to look. This made him very happy, and he took it home. Then he asked the carver, "What do I owe you for making this?" and he replied, "Do as you please about it." The carver had felt sorry to see how this chief was mourning for his wife, so he said, "It is because I felt badly for you that I made that. So don't pay me too much." He paid the carver very well, however, both in slaves and in goods.

Now the chief dressed this image in his wife's clothes and her marten-skin robe. He felt that his wife had come back to him and treated the image just like her. One day, while he sat mourning very close to the image, he felt it move. His wife had also been very fond of him. At first he thought that the movement was only his imagination, yet he watched it every day, for he thought that at some time it would come to life. When he ate he always had the image close to him.

Some time later, however, the image gave forth a sound from its chest like that of crackling wood, and the man knew that it was ill. When he had someone move it away from the place where it had been sitting they found a small cedar tree growing there on top of the flooring. They left it until it grew very large and it is because of this that cedars on the Queen Charlotte Islands are so good. When people up this way look for red cedars and find a good one they say, "This looks like the baby of the chief's wife."

Every day the image of the young woman grew more like a human being, and, when they heard the story, people from villages far and near came in to look at it and at the young cedar tree growing there, at which they were very much astonished. The woman moved around very little and never got to talk, but her husband dreamed what she wanted to tell him. It was through his dreams that he knew she was talking to him.

John R. Swanton, *Tlingit Myths and Texts*, pp. 181-2.

THREE SONGS FROM THE NORTHWEST
(TLINGIT)

1. Song of Cg'watc

I always think within myself
That there is no place
Where people do not die.

I do not know where my dear one is.
Perhaps the spirits threw down my dear
Into the spirit's cave around the world.

2. Song of the Poet

It is only crying about myself
that comes to me in song.

3. Song of Hummingbird

. . . I am feeling very lonely away.
I am singing inside.
I am crying about myself.

From *ibid.*, pp. 401, 410, 412.

TWO MOURNING SONGS FROM THE NORTHWEST

(TLINGIT)

1. Song of Here-is-a-feather

Help me with your believing, Kágrantan's children.
It is as if my grandfather's house were turning over
with me.
Where is the person that will save me?

2. Song of Other-water

My younger brother has brought me a great joy of
laughter.
If I knew the way the spirits go, I would go right to
him.

From *ibid.*, p. 408.

SPEECHES DELIVERED AT A FEAST WHEN A POLE WAS ERECTED FOR THE DEAD

(TLINGIT)

Some morning just at daylight the chief who is about to erect the pole and give the feast, no matter how great a chief he is, passes along in the front of the houses of the town, singing mourning songs for the dead. Then the people know what is wrong and feel badly for him. The memorial pole seems to bring every recollection of the dead back to him. Now is the time when the story of the Raven is used.

After that the chief stands in a place from which he can be heard all over the village. . . . Then he will perhaps speak as follows: "My father's brothers, my grandfathers, people that I came from, my ancestors, my mother's grandfathers, years ago they say that this world was without daylight. Then one person knew that there was daylight with Nas-cáki-yel, and went quickly to his daughter. When he was born he cried for the daylight his grandfather had. Then his grandfather gave it to him. At that time his grandchild brought daylight out upon the poor people he had made in the world. He pitied them. This is the way with me. Darkness is upon me. My mind is sick. Therefore I am now begging daylight from you, my grandfathers, my father's brothers, people I came from, my ancestors, my mother's grandfathers. Can it be that you will give the daylight as Nas-cáki-yel gave it to his grandchild, so that day will dawn upon me?"

[Then the people to whom he is speaking will an-

swer: *"Ye Kugwati,"* that means: "We will make it so."
By "being in the dark" he means that the pole is not
yet raised and he tells them that they will give him
daylight by raising it.]

After it is raised he says: "You have brought day-
light on me." After this speech all show the greatest
respect to this chief and keep very quiet. They do not
allow the children to say anything out of the way.

The evening of the day when the pole is erected
they have a dance. . . .

After this dance the widower, or one of the widow's
family, might rise and speak as follows: "In the first
time took place the flood of Nas-cáki-yel. What the
people went through was pitiful. Their uncle's houses
and their uncle's poles all drifted away. At that time,
however, Old-woman-underneath took pity and made
the flood subside. You were like this while you were
mourning. Your uncle's houses and poles were flooded
over. They drifted away from this world. But now
your grandfathers make it go down like Old-woman-
underneath. You were as if dying with cold from what
had happened to you. Your floor planks too, were all
standing up from the flood. But now they have been
put down. A fire has been made . . . hoping that it
will make you warm."

Then the man who is putting up the pole rises and
says: "I thank you, my grandfathers, for your words.
It is as if I had been in a great flood. But now your
words have made the flood go down from me. My un-
cle's houses have drifted ashore and have been left at
a good place. Your kind words have put down my
floor planks. We have been as if we were cold. But
now that you have made a fire, we shall be warm.

Thank you for what you have done. On account of
your words we will not mourn any more. This is all."

From *ibid.*, pp. 374-7. (Obtained from Katishan at Wran-
gell.) The story of the Raven to which the chief in his
speech refers is the creation myth of the Tlingit, in which
the deeds of the Creator, Nas-cáki-yel, the invisible deity,
and those of the culture hero Yel (Raven), are related.
Here the myth of the beginning of all things is narrated in
order to restore life and to bridge the gap torn open by
death, indicating thus the very essence of all myth-relating
as a magic performance *in se*.

SECTION SEVEN:

From the Far North

IMPROVISED SONG OF JOY
(IGLULIK ESKIMO)

Ajaja—aja—jaja,
The lands around my dwelling
Are more beautiful
From the day
When it is given me to see
Faces I have never seen before.
All is more beautiful,
All is more beautiful,
And life is thankfulness.
These guests of mine
Make my house grand,
Ajaja—aja—jaja.

From Knud Rasmussen, *The Intellectual Culture of the Iglulik Eskimos,* p. 27. The old woman Takomaq, who was about to serve a meal she had prepared for Knud Rasmussen and his companion, was so pleased at the sight of the tea Rasmussen contributed that she at once joyfully improvised the above song.

FROM THE CHILDHOOD MEMORIES OF
THE ESKIMO WOMAN TAKOMAQ

(Iglulik Eskimo)

. . . . Thus I began to live my life. And I reached the age where I was as if awake, and sometimes as if asleep. I could begin to remember. . . .

One day, I remember, I saw a party of children out at play, and I wanted to run out at once and play with them. But my father, who understood hidden things, perceived that I was playing with the souls of my dead brothers and sisters. He was afraid that might be dangerous, and therefore called up his helping spirits and asked them about it. Through his helping spirits my father learned that despite the manner in which I was born, with the aid of a magic bird, and the way my life had been saved by powerful spirits, there was yet something in my soul of that which had brought about the death of all my brothers and sisters. For this reason the dead were often about me, and I could not distinguish between the spirits of the dead and real live people. Thus it was that I had gone out to play with the souls of my dead brothers and sisters, but it was a dangerous thing to do, for in the end, the dead ones might keep me among themselves. My father's helping spirits would therefore now endeavor to protect me more effectively than hitherto, and my father was not to be afraid of my dying now. And after that, whenever I wanted to go out and play with the spirit children, which I always took for real ones, a sort of rocky wall rose up out of the ground, so that I could not get near them. . . .

From *ibid.*, pp. 24-5.

296

SHAMANS AND THEIR TRAINING

As Told by Igjugarjuk

(CARIBOU ESKIMO)

When I was to be a shaman, I chose suffering through the two things that are most dangerous to us humans, suffering through hunger and suffering through cold. . . .

My instructor was my wife's father, Perqanaq. When I was to be exhibited to Pinga and Hila [deities], he dragged me on a little sledge that was no bigger than I just could sit on it; he dragged me far over on the other side of Hikoligjuaq. . . . It was in wintertime and took place at night with the new moon; one could just see the very first streak of the moon; it had just appeared in the sky. I was not fetched again until the next moon was of the same size. Perqanaq built a small snow hut being no bigger than that I could just get under cover and sit down. I was given no sleeping skin to protect me against the cold, only a little piece of caribou skin to sit upon. There I was shut in. The entrance was closed with a block, but no soft snow was thrown over the hut to make it warm. When I sat there five days, Perqanaq came with water, tepid, wrapped in caribou skin, a watertight caribou-skin bag. Not until fifteen days afterwards did he come again and hand me the same, just giving himself time to hand it to me, and then he was gone again, for even the old shaman must not interrupt my solitude. . . . As soon as I had become alone, Perqanaq enjoined me to think of only one thing all the time I was to be there, to want only one single thing, and that was to draw Pinga's attention to the fact that there I sat and wished to be a shaman: Pinga should own me. My novitiate took place in the coldest winter, and I, who never got anything to warm me, and must not move, was very cold, and it was so tiring having to sit without daring to lie down, that sometimes it was as if I died a little. Only towards the end of the thirty days did a helping spirit come to me, a lovely and beautiful helping spirit, whom I had never thought of; it was a white woman; she came to me while I had collapsed, exhausted, and was sleeping. But still I saw her lifelike, hovering over me, and from that day I could not close my eyes or dream without seeing her. There is this remarkable thing about my helping spirit, that I have never seen her while awake, but only in dreams. She came to me from Pinga and was a sign that Pinga had now noticed me and would give me powers that would make me a shaman.

When a new moon was lighted and had the same size as the one that had shone for us when we left the village, Perqanaq came again with his little sledge and . . . dragged me home in the same manner as he had dragged me to Kingarjuit. . . .

For a whole year I was not to lie with my wife, who, however, had to make my food. For a whole year I had to have my own little cooking pot and my own meat dish; no one else was allowed to eat of what had been cooked for me.

Later, when I had quite become myself again, I understood that I had become the shaman of my village, and it did happen that my neighbors or people from

298

a long distance away called me to heal a sick person, or to inspect a course if they were going to travel. When this happened, the people of my village were called together and I told them what I had been asked to do. Then I left tent or snow house and went out into solitude: away from the dwellings of man, but those who remained behind had to sing continuously, just to keep themselves happy and lively. If anything difficult had to be found out, my solitude had to extend over three days and two nights, or three nights and two days. In all that time I had to wander about without rest, and only sit down once in a while on a stone or a snowdrift. When I had been out long and had become tired, I could almost doze and dream what I had come out to find and about which I had been thinking all the time. Every morning, however, I could come home and report on what I had so far found out, but as soon as I had spoken I had to return again, out into the open, out to places where I could be quite alone. In the time when one is out seeking, one may eat a little, but not much. If a shaman out of the secrets of solitude finds out that the sick person will die, he can return home and stay there without first having allowed the usual time to pass. It is only in cases of a possible cure that he must remain out the whole time.

We shamans in the interior have no special spirit language and believe that the real *angatkut* do not need it. On my travels I have sometimes been present at a séance among the salt-water dwellers. These *angatkut* never seemed trustworthy to me. It always appeared to me that these salt-water *angatkut* attached more weight to tricks that would astonish the audience, when they jumped about the floor and lisped all sorts of absurdities and lies in their so-called spirit language; to me all this seemed only amusing and as something that would impress the ignorant. A real shaman does not jump about the floor and do tricks, nor does he seek by the aid of darkness, by putting out the lamps, to make the minds of his neighbors uneasy. For myself, I do not think I know much, but I do not think that wisdom or knowledge about things that are hidden can be sought in that manner. True wisdom is only to be found far away from people, out in the great solitude, and is not found in play but only through suffering. Solitude and suffering open the human mind, and therefore a shaman must seek his wisdom there.

From Knud Rasmussen, *Observations on the Intellectual Culture of the Caribou Eskimos,* pp. 52-4. A few repetitions omitted.

THE LAND OF HEAVEN
(CARIBOU ESKIMO)

Heaven is a great land. In that land there are many holes. These holes we call stars. In the land of heaven lives Pana [the Woman-up-there]. There is a mighty spirit, and the *angatkut* hold that it is a woman. To her pass the souls of the dead. And sometimes, when many die, there are many people up there. When anything is spilt up there, it pours out through the stars and becomes rain or snow. The souls of the dead are reborn in the dwellings of Pana and brought down to earth again by the moon. When the moon is absent, and cannot be seen in the sky, it is because it is busy helping Pana by bringing souls to earth. Some become human beings once more, others become animals, all manner of beasts. And so life goes on without end.

From *ibid.*, p. 79. Told by Kibkarjuk.

ULIVFAK'S SONG OF THE CARIBOU
(Caribou Eskimo)

Eye—aya
I call to mind
And think of the early coming of spring
As I knew it
In my younger days.
Was I ever such a hunter!
Was it myself indeed?
For I see
And recall in memory a man in a kayak;
Slowly he toils along in toward the shores
    of the lake,
With many spear-slain caribou in tow.
Happiest am I
In my memories of hunting in kayak.
On land, I was never of great renown
Among the herds of caribou.
And an old man, seeking strength in his
    youth,
Loves most to think of the deeds
Whereby he gained renown.

From *ibid.*, p. 70. Ulivfak was old, and in his grief at
having lost the agility of his youth, he felt inclined to weep,
but sang this song instead.

DANCE SONG

(Copper Eskimo)

I am quite unable
To capture seals as they do, I am quite unable.
Animals with blubber since I do not know how to
    capture,
To capture seals as they do I am quite unable.
I am quite unable
To shoot as they do, I am quite unable.
I am quite unable,
A fine kayak such as they have I am quite unable to
    obtain.
Animals that have fawns since I cannot obtain them,
A fine kayak such as they have I am quite unable to
    obtain.
I am quite unable
To capture fish as they do, I am quite unable.
Small fish since I cannot capture them,
To capture fish as they do I am quite unable.
I am quite unable
To dance as they do, I am quite unable.
Dance songs since I do not know them at all,
To dance as they do I am quite unable.
I am quite unable to be swift-footed as they are,
I am quite unable. . . .

From Roberts and Jenness, *Songs of the Copper Eskimo*,
pp. 9, 12. The dance house, with the Copper Eskimo, is
the center of social life. Every notable incident, every im-
portant experience or emotion in the daily life is recorded

in a dance song, which takes the place to some extent of the local newspaper. Every Eskimo, whether man or woman, can not only sing and dance, but can even in some measure compose dance songs. Distinction in this field ranks almost as high as distinction in hunting. A man who knows how to make a song is a very valuable adjunct to the community.

UTITIÁQ'S SONG
(Cumberland Sound Eskimo)

Aja, I am joyful; this is good!
Aja, there is nothing but ice around me, that
    is good!
Aja, I am joyful; this is good!
My country is nothing but slush, that is good!
Aja, I am joyful; this is good!
Aja, when, indeed, will this end? This is good!
I am tired of watching and waking, this is good!

From Franz Boas, *Eskimo Tales and Songs,* p. 50. Re-
corded at Cumberland Sound. This song was composed, says
Boas, by a young man named Utitiáq, who went adrift on
the ice when sealing, and did not reach the shore until
after a week of hardships and privations.

SECTION EIGHT:

From Mexico

PRAYER TO THE GOD TITLACAOAN
(AZTEC)

O god all powerful, who gives life to men and whose name is Titlacaoan, do me the favor to grant me what I need to eat and drink and to enjoy your tranquillity and delight, because I live in dire affliction and need in this world. Have mercy because I am so poor and sparsely clad, and I work to serve you, and in this your service I sweep, clean, and light the fire in the hearth of this poor house, where I am awaiting what might be your pleasure to ordain me. O, let me die at once and thus end this troublesome and miserable life, so that I may rest and my body may be at ease.

From Bernardino de Sahagun, *A History of Ancient Mexico*, p. 178.

LAMENTATION

(Aztec)

1.

I lift my voice in wailing, I am afflicted, as I remember that we must leave the beautiful flowers, the noble songs; let us enjoy ourselves for a while, let us sing, for we must depart forever, we are to be destroyed in our dwelling place.

2.

Is it indeed known to our friends how it pains and angers me that never again can they be born, never again be young on this earth.

3.

Yet a little while with them here, then nevermore shall I be with them, nevermore enjoy them, nevermore know them.

4.

Where shall my soul dwell? Where is my home? Where shall be my house? I am miserable on earth.

5.

We take, we unwind the jewels, the blue flowers are woven over the yellow ones, that we may give them to the children.

6.

Let my soul be draped in various flowers; let it be
intoxicated by them; for soon must I weeping go be-
fore the face of our Mother.

From Daniel G. Brinton, *Ancient Nahuatl Poetry*, p. 79.
It is only hesitatingly that I bring specimens of Brinton's
translation into this collection, the aim of which is to set
before the reader, in the main, translations as literal as pos-
sible; having in mind E. Seler's severe criticism of Brinton's
all too sweeping trànslations, the compiler compared his
work with *literal* translations of similar poetical products of
the ancient Mexicans and thus came to the conclusion that
Brinton—with the genius of a poet—must have caught the
atmosphere of this unique literature almost to perfection,
regardless of philological errors with which his translations
might abound.

A SONG OF EXHORTATION BECAUSE CERTAIN ONES DID NOT WANT TO GO TO WAR

(AZTEC)

1.

I strike on my drum, I the skillful singer, that I may arouse, that I may fire our friends, who think of nothing, to whose minds, plunged in sleep, the dawn has not appeared, over whom are yet spread the dark clouds of night; may I not call in vain and poorly, may they hear this song of the rosy dawn, poured abroad widely by the drum, *ohe! ohe!*

2.

The divine flowers of dawn blossom forth, the war flowers of the Cause of All; glittering with dew they scatter abroad their fragrance; bring them hither that they be not hidden nor bloom in vain, that they may rejoice you, our friends, and not in vain shall be the flowers, the living, colored, brilliant flowers.

3.

O youths, here there are skilled men in the flowers of shields, in the flowers of the pendant eagle plumes, the yellow flowers which they grasp; they pour forth noble songs, noble flowers; they make payment with their blood, with their bare breasts; they seek the bloody field of war. And you, O friends, put on your black paint for war, for the path of victory; let us lay hand on our shields, and raise aloft our strength and courage.

From *ibid.*, p. 81.

A SONG BY NEZAHUALCOYOTL

(AZTEC)

1.

The sweet-voiced *quetzal* there, ruling the earth,
has intoxicated my soul.

2.

I am like the quetzal bird, I am created in the one
and only God; I sing sweet songs among the flowers;
I chant songs and rejoice in my heart.

3.

The fuming dewdrops from the flowers in the fields
intoxicate my soul.

4.

I grieve to myself that ever this dwelling on earth
should end.

5.

I foresaw, being a Mexican, that our rule began to
be destroyed, I went forth weeping that it was to bow
down and to be destroyed.

6.

Let me not be angry that the grandeur of Mexico
is to be destroyed.

7.

The smoking stars gather against it; the one who cares for flowers is about to be destroyed.

8.

He who cared for books wept, he wept for the beginning of the destruction.

From *ibid.,* p. 123. The destruction of the Mexican state was foreshadowed by a series of omens and prodigies which took place during the ten years preceding the arrival of Cortes. By the "smoking stars" is meant a comet that was visible for about a year.

315

LOVE SONG
(Aztec)

I know not whether thou hast been absent:
I lie down with thee, I rise up with thee,
In my dreams thou art with me.
If my eardrops tremble in my ears,
I know it is thou moving within my heart.

From Daniel G. Brinton, "Native American Poetry," in
Essays of an Americanist, p. 295. This song was obtained
from the lips of an Indian girl in the Sierra of Tamaulipas.

ABOUT THE EDUCATION OF THE PRIESTS IN ANCIENT MEXICO

(AZTEC)

The first rule was that all those ministers of the idols who were called Tlamacazque were to sleep in the house of Calmecac. The second rule was that they all swept and cleaned that house at four o'clock in the morning. The third one was that the already bigger boys had to go out to look for and gather maguey points [thorns]; the fourth rule was for still older boys to bring in firewood on their backs from the forest; this wood was needed for the fires which were lighted every night; and when any construction work in clay was to be done, be it building walls, ditches, watering canals, or field work, they all went together at daybreak, only those who had to watch the house and those who had to carry the food to the workers, were remaining; no one ever lagged behind, and they all worked with great discipline and good order. The fifth rule was to stop work somewhat early; they then went at once to their monastery to be in charge of the services of their gods and to perform penance exercises and, first of all, to bathe. At sunset they began to get all the necessary things ready, then at eleven o'clock at night, they went on their way, *each one alone by himself,* carrying the points of maguey, a shell on which to play a tune on the road, an incensory of clay, a pouch or bag in which to carry the incense, torches. . . . Thus each one went out naked to deposit the maguey thorns *at his particular place of devotion,* and

317

those who wanted to do very severe penance went far towards the forests, mountains, and rivers. . . . The sixth rule was that the ministers of the idols . . . slept apart, everyone by himself. The seventh rule was that the meals that were consumed there had to be prepared in the house of the Calmecac, because they had a communal income which they spent in food, and if to anyone food was brought from his home, they all shared it. The eighth rule was that every midnight all had to get up *to pray,* and he who did not awake and rise was punished by pricking with points of maguey leaves . . . that he might take warning. The ninth rule was that no one should be overbearing, or offend one another, nor should anyone be disobedient to the order and customs they observed, and if at one time or another one of them appeared intoxicated, or should live in concubinage, or commit some criminal act, they killed him outright, executed him with garrot, roasted him alive, or shot arrows at him. . . . [Another] rule was to teach [the boys] all the verses of the songs to sing; these verses were written in their books by signs; furthermore, they taught them Indian astrology and the interpretation of dreams and the counting of years. . . .

From Sahagun, *op. cit.,* pp. 200-2. Though the diction is Sahagun's, it is nevertheless his Indian informant who has dictated the above account of the rules of monastic education in ancient Mexico.

NOÉH

The Story of the Biblical Flood

(ZAPOTEC)

There was a man called Noéh who was much re-
spected by the people. As Noéh was a Catholic he
went to church. He did not forget God, nor was he for-
saken by God. God sent him a letter. The angel came
down from the sky and gave it to him at seven at
night. The letter said that if the people did not go to
church God was going to put an end to the world.
The people were unmannerly and gross. Noéh was to
hold a meeting so that all might hear that if they did
not go to church, God would put an end to the world.
The people were to give heed to Noéh. Sunday morn-
ing Noéh went with his letter to the town hall, to the
president. When Noéh arrived, he gave the letter to
the secretary, who was writing. All assembled to hear
what Noéh had to say, also to hear the letter. The
secretary said, "God says that you are to hold mass and
to pray, if not, *gyeb Dios, el santo Dios,* will put an
end to the world." They laughed. "Noéh is crazy!"
They did not believe God sent the letter. "Noéh him-
self sent the letter. Noéh is crazy. Let us kill him!"
Noéh said, "I am going. I will explain to God that
you do not believe what he says. I am going." At seven
at night the angel came again. The angel was Gabriel.
He asked, "What do they say, those of the town?"
"They are going to kill me because I am crazy. They
do not believe what the letter says."

"*Sta bueno!* Go and see them again, and if they still

do not believe, God will put an end to the world next week."

The next day, Noéh went to the president and said, "I come again. Excuse me for disturbing you, Señor Presidente. Is it true that you do not believe that God said he would put an end to the world? If you do not believe that God is in the sky he says he will end the world."

"*Bueno,* I believe it," said the president, "but the people do not believe it."

The people assembled again. "Let God do what he wants! We do not believe."

"Well, I will tell him that it is true that you do not believe. But pray a little to God to forgive us."

"No, let God do what he wants! We are not going to church. We do not think there is a God."

"Well, I will tell him."

The angel came again and asked what they said. "They do not believe in God in Heaven."

Said the angel, "Now God will be angry."

Saturday night the angel came down again to the house of Noéh. "God says that now you are to make a boat, as big as a train, and finish it in a week. God is very angry that the townspeople do not believe in him."

So Noéh paid carpenters to make the boat, and at the end of the week it was ready. The people went to look at the boat. "Noéh is crazy! That is why he is making a boat!"

By Sunday the boat was finished. "You have finished your work," said the angel.

"Yes," said Noéh, "I have finished my work."

"God has sent you another letter."

The letter said, "You are to take pains to bring together a pair of crows, a pair of vultures, a pair of little parroquets, a pair of turtledoves, a pair of little parrots, a pair of macaws, a pair of hummingbirds, a pair of rabbits, a pair of hares, a pair of deer, a pair of coyotes, a pair of eagles, a pair of turkeys, a pair of horses, a pair of burros, a pair of all the animals there are in the world, so the world may be replenished, and with all these animals you are to fill the boat." Noéh put a stack of corn into the boat.

Now it began to rain very hard, day and night, for a week. The water rose three meters, the boat began to stir. At the end of fifteen days the water was ten meters high, and the boat was two meters up. Now the houses were falling down because of the water. The people were crying out, "Noéh, please let us come into your boat! We will pay you!" But the boat was closed. Harder and harder fell the rains. At the end of three weeks the houses had disappeared. The waters lasted a month; no longer were the little mountains, like the one you see there [pointing to Yux, the fortified peak], to be seen. In the mountains the trees and the rocks were weeping, since they were alone. The sea was making an end to the world.

Now San Miguel the Archangel came forth and blew his trumpet at the four corners of the sky. "Be it heard in the world that now is the appointed day!" The boat mounted higher. Now Noéh was about to reach the sky, by the road to the north; he stopped at the foot of the sky where there was a big mountain. On top of this mountain he stopped. *Duri duri duri* [speedily] the water began to dry up. The wind came, leveling the world, all the mountains fell down, the world was a plain.

There came another letter to Noéh. "Look, Noéh, you are to send out the birds in pairs to see if the world is drying up."

First to go forth was the vulture. He found cattle dead in the mud. He stayed to eat and brought back no report to Noéh. Crow went forth. When he came back he said, "Now the earth is ready to sow, so that there may be ears of corn." Forth went turtledove. He returned, saying that the water was only up to his leg —he has a very small leg, he is very small. Forth went parroquet. He came back and said, "Now the world is dry, now it is all right for the servant girl to bring us bread." Then all the animals went forth to look for a living. There came another letter to Noéh: "Now you can go forth with all your family. There is going to be a smoke in the world for the world to begin again."

The boat rested on top of a big mountain. Noéh found a big pine tree. From a big hole in it a person came out. He had survived the water, only he and Noéh and his family. Then Noéh made himself another house and ranch.

From Elsie Clews Parsons, *Mitla, Town of the Souls,* p. 350. An interesting study, dedicated to the problem of Indian-Spanish relationships.

THE EAGLE AND THE MOON GODDESS

A Song from the Fertility Rites

(Cora)

Under the sky the eagle, there he abides, there far
above us.
Beautiful he appears.
In his talons he holds his world.
A gray garment he wears, a beautiful, living-moist
garment of clouds.
There he waits for the words of Tētewan.
Bright-eyed he looks down upon his world.
Towards the west his eyes are turned.
Bright-eyed he looks down upon the waters of life.
His countenance radiates calamity.
Magnificent is his eye, the sun!
Red are his feet.

There he abides, far away, above us.
There he remembers those who live on this earth.
Wide he spreads his wings over the earth.
And beneath his wings the gods grant rain, the gods
grant dew.
Dew of life comes forth here on earth.
His voice rises, above us.
It is we who hear it, lovely are the words. . . .
Tētewan even hears them, she who abides in the
underworld.
There the Mother hears him.
And she responds; here we listen to the words of
Tētewan.

Here they meet with the words of the eagle, here they
  mingle.

  The words of the eagle fade away, far above the
    waters of life
There, the words of the Mother drift . . .
There they die away, far yonder, beneath the dome
    of the sky.
Far yonder the words vanish.

From K. T. Preuss, *Die Religion der Cora Indianer,* p. 43.

THE CREATION

(UITOTO, COLOMBIA)

1.

A phantasm, nothing else existed in the beginning;
the Father touched an illusion, he grasped something
mysterious. Nothing existed. Through the agency of
a dream our Father Naimuena [he who is or has a
phantasm] kept the mirage to his body, and he pon-
dered long and thought deeply.

2.

Nothing existed, not even a stick to support the vi-
sion: our Father attached the illusion to the thread
of a dream and kept it by the aid of his breath. He
sounded to reach the bottom of the appearance, but
there was nothing. Nothing existed indeed.

3.

Then the Father again investigated the bottom of
the mystery. He tied the empty illusion to the dream
thread and pressed the magical substance upon it.
Thus by the aid of his dream he held it like a wisp of
raw cotton.

4.

Then he seized the mirage bottom and stamped
upon it repeatedly, sitting down at last on his dreamed
earth.

The earth-phantasm was now his, and he spat out saliva repeatedly so that the forests might grow. Then he lay down upon his earth and covered it with the roof of heaven. As he was the owner of the earth he placed above it the blue and the white sky.

6.

Thereupon, Rafuema, "the man who has the narratives," sitting at the base of the heavens, pondered, and he created this story so that we might listen to it here upon earth.

Translated from K. T. Preuss, *Die Religion und Mythologie der Uitoto*, pp. 166 ff. The Uitoto of Colombia are, in all their actions, thoughts, and dreams, guided by the mysterious moon processes of growing, waning, and regrowing. The divine being they revere most deeply is a representation not of the unchangeable absolute, but of the processes of becoming, dying, and resurrection. The earth is a creation of the moon.

SECTION NINE:

From Central America

A MAYA PROPHECY

(Yucatán)

Eat, eat, while there is bread,
Drink, drink, while there is water;
A day comes when dust shall darken the air,
When a blight shall wither the land,
When a cloud shall arise,
When a mountain shall be lifted up,
When a strong man shall seize the city,
When ruin shall fall upon all things,
When the tender leaf shall be destroyed,
When eyes shall be closed in death;
When there shall be three signs on a tree,
Father, son, and grandson hanging dead on the
    same tree;
When the battle flag shall be raised,
And the people scattered abroad in the forests.

Translated from D. G. Brinton, "The Books of Chilam
Balam," in *Essays of an Americanist*, p. 303. The Books of
Chilam Balam are the sacred books of the Maya of Yucatán
and were named after their last prophet, Balam, who lived
during the last decades of the fifteenth century and fore-
told the coming of strangers from the east who would bring
with them a new religion. The prompt fulfillment of his
prediction enhanced greatly his reputation as a prophet,
and prophecies uttered long before his time were later
ascribed to his authority. In these Books of Chilam Balam
we find besides prophecies, rituals, mythological accounts
of the creation of the world, purely Mayan in origin, mate-
rial which is clearly European.

THREE FRAGMENTS FROM THE BOOK
OF CHILAM BALAM CHUMAYEL
(Maya)

1.

. . . It was only because these priests of ours were to come to an end when misery was introduced, when Christianity was introduced by the real Christians. Then with the true God, the true Dios, came the beginning of our misery. It was the beginning of tribute, the beginning of church dues, . . . the beginning of strife with blow-guns, the beginning of strife by trampling on people, the beginning of robbery by violence . . . a beginning of vexation. This was the origin of service to the Spaniards and priests, of service to the public prosecutors . . . while the poor people were harassed.

2.

They [the great Itzá] did not wish to join with the foreigners; they did not desire Christianity. They did not wish to pay tribute . . . Four hundreds of years and fifteen score years was the end of their lives; then came the end of their lives; because they knew the measure of their days. Complete was the month; complete the year; complete the night; complete the breath of life as it passed also. . . . In due measure did they recite the good prayers; in due measure they sought the lucky days, until they saw the good stars enter into their reign; then they kept watch while the reign of the good stars began. Then everything was good. Then they adhered to the dictates of their reason. . . . The foreigners made it otherwise when they arrived here. . . .

3.

. . . Give yourself up, my younger brothers, my older brothers, submit to the unhappy destiny of the Katun which is to come. If you do not submit, you shall be moved from where your feet are rooted. If you do not submit, you shall gnaw the trunks of trees and herbs. If you do not submit, I shall be as when the deer die, so that they go forth from your settlement. . . . If you surrender yourselves, you shall follow Christ, when he shall come. Then his visitation shall end. Then shall come to pass the shaking of the Plumeria flower. Then you shall understand. Then it shall thunder from the dry sky. Then shall be spoken that which is written on the wall. Then you shall set up God, that is, you shall admit his divinity to your hearts. I hardly know what wise man among you will understand. He who understands will go into the forest to serve Christianity. Who will understand it?

From Ralph L. Roys, *The Book of Chilam Balam Chumayel*, pp. 78, 83, 122. "The missionaries caused much suffering by forcibly moving country people from their homes and collecting them in towns to facilitate their conversion to Christianity."

The arrival of the Spaniards under Francisco Montejo in the year 1542 sounded, as Sylvanus G. Morley says, the death knell of all native institutions. The Spanish priests were eager to convert the heathen as speedily as possible; and to do so they thought it necessary first to destroy ruthlessly that which was dearest to the hearts of the Maya:

331

their hieroglyphic manuscripts. The sorrow of a whole race, doomed to spiritual death, expressed itself in these *Books of Chilam Balam,* which preserve for us all that we know of the ancient history of Yucatán. "These manuscripts were written in the Maya language with the letters of the Spanish alphabet . . . the literary instinct of the Maya people, abruptly checked in purely native channels of expression such as the hieroglyphics, seems to have sought relief in this new writing, which had been prepared by the priesthood to facilitate conversion."

It was within fifty years of the Conquest that there came to be quite a number of these *Books of Chilam Balam,* most of which have much to recommend them, according to Sylvanus Morley, as reliable sources for the reconstruction of Maya history. The Chumayel manuscript, however, is to be considered not so much as a historical chronicle but rather as a moving chant of sorrow and distress. See Sylvanus G. Morley, *The Historical Value of the Books of Chilam Balam.*

PRAYER BEFORE PREPARING THE MILPA
(MAYA)

In the name of the Father, the Son, and the Holy Spirit, Amen. Here I stand. Three times before you I stand. I bow down to God the Father, God the Son, and God the Holy Spirit. Behold, my Lord, how I stand in your presence, God, and in the presence of the Lords of the Forests. Forgive me my sins. That you may not forget me without cause I offer these five calabashes of *posol* in order that the big men, the Lords of the Forest, who are the true Lords, may drink. The Lords of the Forest pass before to clear the roads. Behold, my Lord, the good intentions in the presence of the gods. I am making this drinking-offering for my milpa. Forgive me, O my great masters. Accept then but one cool draught of *posol* that the anger that is in your heart [toward me] may be cooled. In the name of God the Master, God the Son, God the Holy Ghost. Amen.

From J. Eric Thompson, *The Mayas of Southern and Central British Honduras,* p. 115. A strong influence of Christianity is apparent, yet the Lords of the Forest are the "true Lords." The Milpa is the field of the Maya which has been wrestled from the suffocating growth of the virgin forest by burning down the trees.

A LETTER BY FRANCISCO DE MONTEJO XIU, 1567

(MAYA)

After we learned the good, in knowing God our Lord as the only true God, leaving our blindness and idolatries, and Your Majesty as temporal lord, before we could well open our eyes to the one and the other, there came upon us a persecution of the worst that can be imagined; and it was in the year '62, on the part of the Franciscan religious, who had taken us to teach the doctrine, instead of which they began to torment us, hanging us by the hands and whipping us cruelly, hanging weights of stone on our feet, torturing many of us in a windlass, giving the torture of the water, from which many died or were maimed.

Being in these tribulations and burdens, trusting in Your Majesty's Justice to hear and defend us, there came the Dr. Quijada to aid our tormentors, saying that we were idolators and sacrificers of men, and many other things against all truth, which we never committed during our time of blindness and infidelity. And as we see ourselves maimed by cruel tortures, many dead of them, robbed of our property, and yet more, seeing disinterred the bones of our baptized ones, who died as Christians, we came to despair.

Not content with this, the religious [i.e. the friars] and the royal Justice held at Mani a solemn auto of inquisition, where they seized many statues, disinterred many dead and burned them there in public; made slaves of many to save Spaniards, . . . the one

334

and the other gave us great wonder and fear, because we did not know what it all was, having been recently baptized, and not informed; and when we returned to our people and told them to hear and guard justice, they seized us, put us in prison and chains, like slaves, in the monastery at Mérida, where many of us died; and they told us we would be burned, without our knowing the why.

At this time came the bishop whom Your Majesty sent, who, although he took us from prison and relieved us from death and the *sambenitos*, has not relieved us from the shame of the charges that were made against us, that we were idolaters, human sacrificers, and had slain many men; because, at the last, he is of the habit of San Francisco and does for them. He has consoled us by his words, saying that Your Majesty would render justice.

A receptor came from Mexico, and made inquiry, and we believe it went to the Audiencia, and nothing has been done.

Then came as governor Don Luis de Céspedes, and instead of relieving us he has increased our burdens, taking away our daughters and wives to serve the Spaniards, against their wills and ours; which we feel so greatly that the common people say that not in the time of our infidelity were we so vexed or maltreated, because our ancestors never took from one his children, nor from husbands their wives to make use of them, as today does Your Majesty's Justice, even to the service of the Negroes and mulattoes.

And with all our afflictions and labors, we have loved the fathers and supplied their necessities, have built many monasteries for them, provided with ornaments and bells, all at our cost and that of our vassals and fellows; although in payment of our services they have made of us their vassals, have deprived us of the signories we inherited from our ancestors, a thing we never suffered in the time of our infidelity. And we obey Your Majesty's Justice, hoping that you will send us remedy.

One thing that has greatly dismayed and stirred us up, is the letters written by Fray Diego de Landa, chief author of all these ills and burdens, saying that Your Majesty has approved the killings, robberies, tortures, slaveries and other cruelties inflicted on us; to which we wonder that such things should be said of so Catholic and upright a king as is Your Majesty. If it is told that we have sacrificed men after we received baptism, it is a great and false witness invented by them to gild their cruelties.

And if there have been or are idols among us, they are but those we have gathered to send to the religious as they required of us, saying that we had confessed to their possession under the torture; but all know that we went many leagues to gather from places where we knew that they had been kept by those before us, and which we had abandoned when we were baptized; and in good conscience they should not punish us as they have done.

If Your Majesty wishes to learn of all, send a person to search the truth, to learn of our innocence and the great cruelty of the *padres;* and had not the bishop come, we should all have been brought to an end. And though we cherish well Fray Diego and the other *padres* who torment us, only to hear them named causes our entrails to revolt. Therefore, Your Majesty, send us other ministers to teach us and preach to us the law of God, for we much desire our salvation.

The religious of San Francisco of this province have written certain letters to Your Majesty and to the general of the order, in praise of Fray Diego and his other companions, who were those who tortured, killed and put us to scandal; and they gave certain letters written in the Castilian language to certain Indians of their familiars, and thus they signed them and sent them to Your Majesty. May Your Majesty understand that they are not ours, we who are chiefs of this land, and who did not have to write lies nor falsehoods nor contradictions. May Fray Diego de Landa and his companions suffer the penance for the evils they have done to us, and may our descendants to the fourth generation be recompensed the great persecutions that came on us.

May God guard Your Majesty for many years in his sacred service and for our good and protection.

From Yucatán, the 12th of April, 1567.

FRANCISCO DE MONTEJO XIU

From William Gates, *Yucatán before and after the Conquest*, pp. 115-7. Fray Diego de Landa, to whom the writer of the above letter repeatedly refers, is famous for having been one of the cruelest missionaries of the Christian faith, and for having written an able account of the Maya culture, the *Relación de las Cosas de Yucatán;* he wrote in Spain, whence he was called on charges of cruelty. Smoothly he goes over the account of the *Auto da fé* where he let go up in flames the sacred books of the Maya, an act which "they took," as he concludes his narrative, "most grievously, and which gave them great pain." Nevertheless, he gained the power of a bishop, and with the blessings of his homelands

337

returned to Yucatán. However, the activities of a Fra Diego de Landa were severely criticized not only by contemporary members of the Franciscan Order but still more so by those of later times; today it is among the Franciscan Fathers that we find some of the most tolerant and understanding anthropologists of our times.

SECTION TEN:

From Peru

SUPPLICATION TO THE CREATOR GOD
(INCA)

Viracocha, Lord of the Universe!
Whether male or female,
at any rate commander of heat and
    reproduction,
being one who,
even with His spittle, can work sorcery.
Where art thou?
Would that thou wert not hidden
    from this son of Thina!
He may be above;
He may be below;
or, perchance, abroad in space.
Where is His mighty judgment seat?
Hear me!
He may be spread abroad among the
    upper waters;
or among the lower waters and their
    sands
He may be dwelling.
Creator of the world,
Creator of man,
great among my ancestors,
before Thee
my eyes fail mè,
though I long to see Thee;
for, seeing Thee,
knowing Thee,
learning from Thee,

understanding Thee,
I shall be seen by Thee,
and Thou wilt know me.
The Sun—the Moon;
the Day—the Night;
Summer—Winter;
not in vain,
in orderly succession,
do they march
to their destined place,
to their goal.
They arrive
wherever
Thy royal staff
Thou bearest.
Oh! Harken to me,
listen to me,
let it not befall
that I grow weary
and die.

From P. Ainsworth Means, *Ancient Civilizations of the Andes,* p. 437. Means, on his part, derived this supplication, "typically Andean in tone and in spirit," from Dr. Miguel Mossi, who translated it into English from the Quechua text, printed in *Lafone Quevedo,* 1892, p. 339.

LOVE SONG FROM THE ANDES
(INCA)

To this my song
Thou shalt sleep.
In the dead of night
I shall come.

From *ibid.*, p. 436. Derived from Garcilaso. In Inca times poetical compositions were verbally perpetuated by professional bards called *haravecs*. The lyrical verse were unrhymed, but either rhythmical or cadenced. The Peruvians were a highly musical people and stand, in this regard, at the forefront of the pre-Spanish peoples of America. The old Andeans used either percussion instruments or wind instruments; most wide-spread was the use of the pan-pipe, made either of reeds or of pottery, the trumpet, fashioned from shell, or from wood, clay, or metal; and flutes of many kinds. (See R. and M. d'Harcourt, *La musique des Incas et ses survivances*.)

PERUVIAN DANCE SONG
(AYACUCHO)

Wake up, woman,
Rise up, woman,
In the middle of the street
A dog howls.

May the death arrive,
May the dance arrive,

Comes the dance
You must dance,
Comes the death
You can't help it!

Ah! what a chill,
Ah! what a wind. . . .

From R. et M.d'Harcourt, *La musique des Incas et ses survivances*, p. 477. The lines of this strange dance song convey a weird feeling of grim joyfulness; the spirit of the medieval *dances macabres* throbs behind these strophes.

Bibliography

TEXT

ALEXANDER, HARTLEY BURR. *L'Art et La Philosophie Des Indiens de L'Amérique du Nord.* Paris: Editions Ernest Leroux, 1926.

BANDELIER, A. F. *Final Report of Investigations among the Indians of the Southwestern United States.* Cambridge, 1890.

BENEDICT, RUTH F. "The Vision in Plains Culture," in *The American Anthropologist,* N. S., 24, 1-2.

——. *The Concept of the Guardian Spirit in North America.* The American Anthropological Association, *Memoirs,* No. 29, 1923.

——. *Patterns of Culture.* Boston and New York: Houghton Mifflin Company, 1934.

——. *Zuñi Mythology. Columbia University Contributions to Anthropology.* New York, 1935.

BOAS, FRANZ. "Literature, Music, and Dance." In *General Anthropology.* Boston: D. C. Heath and Company, 1938.

——. *Race, Language, and Culture.* New York: The Macmillan Company, 1940.

BOGORAS, WALDEMAR. "Primitive Ideas of Space and Time." In *The American Anthropologist,* N. S. 27 (1925).

BUNZEL, RUTH. *The Pueblo Potter. Columbia University Contributions to Anthropology,* Vol. 8. New York: 1929.

345

BUNZEL, RUTH (cont.). *Introduction to Zuñi Ceremonialism.* 47th Annual Report of the Bureau of American Ethnology, Washington, 1930.

BURTON, FREDERICK R. *American Primitive Music.* New York: Moffat, 1909.

CUSHING, FRANK. *Outlines of Zuñi Creation Myths.* 13th Report of the Bureau of American Ethnology, Washington, 1896.

——. *Zuñi Breadstuff.* Museum of the American Indian, Heye Foundation, Vol. 8, New York, 1920.

DENSMORE, FRANCES. *Chippewa Music I, II.* Bureau of American Ethnology, Bulletins, 45, 53. Washington, 1910, 1913.

——. *Teton Sioux Music. Ibid.* 61 (1918).

——. *Mandan and Hidatsa Music. Ibid.* 80 (1923).

——. *Yuman and Yaqui Music. Ibid.* 110 (1932).

——. *Nootka and Quileute Music. Ibid.* 124 (1939).

ESPIÑOSA, J. MANUEL, ed. *First Expedition of De Vargas into New Mexico 1692,* Albuquerque, 1940.

FLETCHER, ALICE, and LAFLESCHE, FRANCIS. *The Omaha Tribe.* 27th Report of the Bureau of American Ethnology, Washington, 1911.

FORDE, C. DARYLL. *Ethnography of the Yuma Indians. University of California Publications in American Archaeology and Ethnology,* Vol. 38. Berkeley, 1931.

GAYTON, ANNA, and NEWMAN, STANLEY S. *Yokuts and Western Mono Myths. Anthropological Records of the University of California,* Vol. 5, No. 1. Berkeley, 1940.

GODDARD, R. P. *Life and Culture of the Hupa. University of California Publications in American Archaeology and Ethnology.* Berkeley, 1903.

HAEBERLIN, K. H. *The Idea of Fertilization in the Culture of the Pueblo Indians.* The American Anthropological Association, *Memoirs,* Vol. 3, Pt. 1. Lancaster, Pa., 1916.

HAILE, FATHER BERARD. *Origin Legend of the Navajo Enemy Way. Yale University Publications in Anthropology.* New Haven, 1938.

HARRIS, JACK S. "The White Knife Shoshoni of Nevada." In R. Linton, ed., *Acculturation in Seven American Indian Tribes.* New York: D. Appleton-Century Company, 1940.

HERSKOVITS, MELVILLE J. *Acculturation, The Study of Culture Contact.* New York, J. J. Augustin, 1938.

HILL, W. W. "Navaho Rites for Dispelling Insanity and Delirium." In *El Palacio,* N. S., XLI, 14-16.

——. *The Agricultural and Hunting Methods of the Navaho Indians. Yale University Publications in Anthropology,* No. 18. New Haven, 1938.

KENTON, EDNA. *The Jesuit Relations and Allied Documents.* New York: A. and C. Boni, 1925.

KLUCKHOHN, CLYDE, and WYMAN, LELAND C. *An Introduction to Navajo Chant Practice.* The American Anthropological Association, *Memoirs.* Menasha, 1940.

KROEBER, A. L. *Handbook of the Indians of California.* Bureau of American Ethnology Bulletin 78. Washington, 1925.

LOWIE, ROBERT H. *The Religion of the Crow Indians. Anthropological Papers of the American Museum of Natural History,* Vol. 25, New York, 1922.

——. *Studies in Plains Indian Folklore. University of California Publications in American Archaeology and Ethnology,* Vol. 40, No. 1. Berkeley, 1932.

347

NEWMAN, STANLEY S. *See* GAYTON, ANNA.

MICHELSON, TRUMAN. *The Owl Sacred Pack of the Fox Indians.* Bureau of American Ethnology, Bulletin 72. Washington, 1921.

PARSONS, ELSIE C. *Mitla, The Town of the Souls.* Chicago: Chicago University Press, 1936.

PREUSS, KONRAD T. *Die Religion und Mythologie der Uitoto.* Leipzig, 1921.

RASMUSSEN, KNUD. *The Intellectual Culture of the Iglulik Eskimo.* Copenhagen, 1929.

REICHARD, GLADYS A. *The Social Life of the Navajo. Columbia University Contributions to Anthropology,* Vol. VII, New York, 1928.

——. *Navajo Medicine Man.* New York: J. J. Augustin, 1939.

SPICER, E. H. *Pascua, A Yaqui Village in Arizona.* Chicago: Chicago University Press, 1940.

SAPIR, EDWARD. "Culture, Genuine and Spurious." In *American Journal for Sociology,* XXIX (1924), 401-417.

——. "Cultural Anthropology and Psychiatry." In *Journal of Abnormal Psychology,* XXVII (1932), 229-42.

——. "The Emergence of the Concept of Personality in a Study of Culture." In *Journal of Social Psychology,* V (1934), 408-15.

SPIER, LESLIE. *Southern Diegueño Customs. University of California Publications in American Archæology and Ethnology,* Vol. 20. Berkeley, 1923.

——. *Yuman Tribes of the Gila River.* Chicago: University of Chicago Press, 1933.

——. *The Prophet Dance of the Northwest and its Derivatives: the Source of the Ghost Dance.* General Series in Anthropology, Vol. I, Pt. 1. Menasha, 1935.

——, and SAPIR, EDWARD. *Wishram Ethnography. University of Washington Publications in Anthropology*, Vol. 3. Washington, 1930.

SPINDEN, HERBERT J. *The Nez Percé Indians*. The American Anthropological Association, *Memoirs*, Vol. 2, 1908.

——. *Songs of the Tewa*. Exposition of Indian Tribal Arts. New York, 1933.

THALBITZER, W. *The Amassalik Eskimo*. Copenhagen: 1923.

THOMPSON, J. ERIC. *The Religious Practices of the Maya of Southern and British Honduras. Field Museum of Natural History, Anthropological Series*, Vol. 27, 1927.

UNDERHILL, RUTH. *Autobiography of a Papago Woman*. The American Anthropological Association, *Memoirs*, Vol. 46, 1936.

——. *Singing for Power, The Song Magic of the Papago Indians of Southern Arizona*. Berkeley, University of California Press, 1938.

WALKER, J. R. *The Sun Dance and Other Ceremonies of the Oglala Division of the Teton Dakota. Anthropological Papers of the American Museum of Natural History*, Vol. 46, 1936.

WHEELWRIGHT, MARY C. *Navajo Creation Myth of the Emergence, By Hasteen Klah. Navajo Religion Series*, Vol. I. Santa Fé: Museum of Navajo Ceremonial Art, 1942.

WHITE, LESLIE A. *The Acoma Indians*. 47th Report of the Bureau of American Ethnology, Washington, 1930.

WHITE, LESLIE A. (cont.). *The Pueblo of San Felipe, New Mexico.* The American Anthropological Association, *Memoirs,* Vol. 38, 1932.

——. *The Pueblo of Santo Domingo, New Mexico.* The American Anthropological Association, *Memoirs,* Vol. 43, 1935.

WISSLER, CLARK. *Ceremonial Bundles of the Blackfoot Indians. Papers of the American Museum of Natural History,* Vol. 7, 1912.

——. *The American Indian, An Introduction to the Anthropology of the New World.* 3rd ed. New York: Oxford University Press, 1938.

ANTHOLOGY

ALEXANDER, HARTLEY BURR. *North American Mythology.* Boston: Marshall Jones Company, 1916.

BENEDICT, RUTH FULTON. *Tales of the Cochiti Indians.* Bureau of American Ethnology, Bulletin 98. Washington, 1931.

BLACK HAWK. *Autobiography of Black Hawk,* as dictated by himself to Antoine LeClair, 1833. Iowa: Historical Society of Iowa. Reprint 1932.

BOAS, FRANZ. *The Ethnology of the Kwakiutl.* 35th Annual Report of the Bureau of American Ethnology. Washington, 1921.

——. "Eskimo Tales and Songs." In *Journal of American Folklore,* VII, 1894.

——. *Folk Tales of Salishan and Sahaptin Tribes.* New York: American Folklore Society, 1917.

——. *The Religion of the Kwakiutl Indians. Columbia University Contributions to Anthropology,* Vol. 10. New York, 1930.

BRINTON, DANIEL G. *Ancient Nahuatl Poetry. Library of American Aboriginal Literature,* Vol. 7. Philadelphia, 1887.

——. "The Books of Chilam Balam." In *Essays of an Americanist.* Philadelphia, 1890.

——. "Native American Poetry." In *Essays of an Americanist,* 1890.

BUNZEL, RUTH L. *Zuñi Katcina: An Analytical Study.* 47th Annual Report of the Bureau of American Ethnology. Washington, 1932.

——. *Zuñi Ritual Poetry.* 47th *Ibid.,* Washington, 1932.

——. *Zuñi Texts. Publications of the American Ethnological Society,* Vol. 15. New York: Stechert, 1933.

BURTON, FREDERICK. *American Primitive Music.* New York: Moffat, 1909.

COOLIDGE, DANE and MARY R. *The Navajo Indians.* Boston and New York: Houghton Mifflin, 1930.

CUSHING, FRANK. *Outlines of Zuñi Creation Myths.* 13th Annual Report of the Bureau of American Ethnology. Washington, 1896.

DELORIA, ELLA. *Dakota Texts. Publications of the American Ethnological Society,* Vol. 14. New York: Stechert, 1932.

DENIG, EDWIN T. *Indian Tribes of the Upper Missouri.* 46th Annual Report of the Bureau of American Ethnology. Washington, 1930.

DENSMORE, FRANCES. *Chippewa Music, I, II.* Bureau of American Ethnology Bulletins 45, 53. Washington, 1910, 1913.

——. *Teton Sioux Music. Ibid.* 61, 1918.

——. *Papago Music. Ibid.* 90, 1929.

——. *Pawnee Music. Ibid.* 93, 1929.

——. *Nootka and Quileute Music. Ibid.* 124, 1939.

DENSMORE, FRANCES (cont.). *Music of Santo Domingo Pueblo, New Mexico. Southwest Museum Papers,* No. 12. Los Angeles, 1938.

D'HARCOURT, RAOUL et MARIE. *La musique des Incas et ses survivances.* Paris, 1925. 2 vol.

DORSEY, GEORGE A. *Traditions of the Skidi Pawnee.* American Folklore Society. Boston and New York: Houghton Mifflin, 1904.

——. *The Traditions of the Caddo.* Washington: Carnegie Institution of Washington, 1905.

——. *The Pawnee Mythology.* Washington: Carnegie Institution of Washington, 1906.

DRAKE, SAMUEL G. *Biography and History of the Indians of North America.* Boston, 1851.

DUBOIS, CONSTANCE GODDARD. "Mythology of the Mission Indians." In *Journal of American Folklore,* Vol. 19, 1906.

——. *The Religion of the Luiseño Indians. University of California Publications in American Archaeology and Ethnology,* Vol. 8. Berkeley, 1908.

DUBOIS, CORA, and DEMETRACOPOULOU, D., *Wintu Myths. University of California Publications in American Archaeology and Ethnology,* Vol. 28, No. 5. Berkeley, 1931.

EASTMAN, CHARLES ALEXANDER. *The Soul of the Indian.* Boston and New York: Houghton Mifflin, 1911.

EGGAN, DOROTHY. "The General Problem of Hopi Adjustment." *The American Anthropologist,* N. S. XLV (1943), 357-73.

FLETCHER, ALICE. *Indian Story and Song from North America.* Boston: Small, Maynard & Co., 1900.

——, and LAFLÉSCHE, FRANCIS. *The Omaha Tribe.* 27th

Annual Report of the Bureau of American Ethnology. Washington, 1911.

FORDE, C. DARYLL. *Ethnography of the Yuma Indians. University of California Publications in American Archaeology and Ethnology*, Vol. 28, No. 4. Berkeley, 1931.

GATES, WILLIAM. *Yucatán before and after the Conquest.* Baltimore: The Maya Society, 1937.

GODDARD, PLINY EARLE. *Gotal: A Mescalero Apache Ceremony.* Putnam Anniversary Volume. New York: Stechert, 1909.

——. *The Masked Dancers of the Apache.* Holmes Anniversary Volume. Washington, 1916.

——. *Navajo Texts. Anthropological Papers of the American Museum of Natural History,* Vol. 34. New York, 1933.

HOIJER, HARRY. *Chiricahua and Mescalero Apache Texts.* With ethnological notes by M. E. Opler. *The University of Chicago Publications in Anthropology, Linguistic Series.* Chicago, 1938.

HALE, HORATIO. *The Iroquois Book of Rites,* Philadelphia, 1883.

JENNESS, DIAMOND. *See* HELEN H. ROBERTS.

KROEBER, A. L. *Handbook of the Indians of California.* Bureau of American Ethnology, Bulletin 78. Washington, 1925.

——. "Wishosk Myths." In *Journal of American Folklore,* Vol. 18, 1905.

LAFLÉSCHE, FRANCIS. *The Osage Tribe: The Rite of Vigil.* 39th Annual Report of the Bureau of American Ethnology. Washington, 1925.

——. *The War Ceremony and Peace Ceremony of the*

Osage Indians. Bureau of American Ethnology, Bulletin 101. Washington, 1939.

LOWIE, ROBERT H. *The Assiniboine. Anthropological Papers of the American Museum of Natural History,* Vol. 4, Pt. 1. Washington, 1909.

——. *The Religion of the Crow Indians. Ibid.,* 25, 1922.

MATTHEWS, WASHINGTON. *Navajo Legends.* The American Folklore Society. Boston and New York: Houghton Mifflin, 1897.

——. *Navajo Myths, Prayers, and Songs. University of California Publications in American Archaeology and Ethnology,* Vol. 5. Berkeley, 1907.

MEANS, PHILIPP AINSWORTH. *Ancient Civilizations of the Andes.* New York: Scribner's, 1931.

MICHELSON, TRUMAN. *The Owl Sacred Pack of the Fox Indians.* Bureau of American Ethnology, Bulletin 72. Washington, 1921.

——. *On the Fox Indians.* 40th Annual Report of the Bureau of American Ethnology. Washington, 1925.

——. *Fox Miscellany.* Bureau of American Ethnology, Bulletin 114. Washington, 1937.

MOONEY, JAMES. *Sacred Formulas of the Cherokees.* 7th Annual Report of the Bureau of American Ethnology. Washington, 1891.

——. *The Ghost Dance Religion and the Sioux Outbreak of 1890.* 14th *ibid.,* 1896.

——. *Myths of the Cherokees,* 19th *ibid.,* 1900.

MORLEY, SYLVANUS. *The Historical Value of the Books of Chilam Balam. Papers of the Archaeological Institute of America,* No. 19, 1911.

NEIHARDT, JOHN G. *Black Elk Speaks, the Life Story of an Oglala Sioux.* New York, 1932.

OPLER, MORRIS EDWARD. *An Apache Life Way, the*

Economic, Social, and Religious Institutions of the Chiricahua Indians. University of Chicago Publications in Anthropology, Ethnological Series. Chicago, 1941.

PARSONS, ELSIE CLEWS. *Mitla, Town of the Souls, Ibid.,* 1936.

PHINNEY, ARCHIE. *Nez Percé Texts. Columbia University Contributions to Anthropology,* Vol. 25. New York, 1934.

PREUSS, KONRAD T. *Die Nayarit-Expedition, Textaufnahmen und Beobachtungen unter Mexikanischen Indianern,* Band I: *Die Religion der Cora Indianer.* Leipzig, 1912.

——. *Die Religion und Mythologie der Uitoto.* Leipzig, 1921.

RADIN, PAUL. *Crashing Thunder, the Autobiography of an American Indian.* New York: D. Appleton Co., 1926.

RASMUSSEN, KNUD. *The Intellectual Culture of the Iglulik Eskimos.* Copenhagen: Gyldendalske boghandel, 1929.

——. *Observations on the Intellectual Culture of the Caribou Eskimos.* Copenhagen, 1930.

ROBERTS, HELEN H., and JENNESS, DIAMOND. *Songs of the Copper Eskimos. Report of the Canadian Arctic Expedition, 1913-1918,* Vol. 14, 1925.

ROYS, RALPH. *The Book of Chilam Balam Chumayel.* Washington: Carnegie Institution of Washington, 1933.

RUSSEL, FRANK. *The Pima Indians.* 26th Annual Report of the Bureau of American Ethnology. Washington, 1904.

SAHAGUN, BERNARDINO DE. *A History of Ancient Mexico.* Translated by Fanny R. Bandelier. Nashville: Fisk University Press, 1932.

SAPIR, EDWARD. *Takelma Texts.* Washington, 1909.

SPECK, FRANK G. *A Study of the Delaware Indian Big House Ceremony. Publications of the Pennsylvania Historical Commission,* Vol. 2. Harrisburg, 1931.

SPIER, LESLIE. *Havasupai Ethnography. Anthropological Papers of the American Museum of Natural History,* Vol. 29. New York, 1928.

——. *Yuman Tribes of the Gila River. University of Chicago Publications in Anthropology, Ethnological Series.* Chicago, 1933.

——. *The Prophet Dance of the Northwest and its Derivatives: The Source of the Ghost Dance. General Series in Anthropology,* Vol. 1. Menasha: 1935.

SPINDEN, HERBERT J. *The Nez Percé Indians.* The American Anthropological Association, *Memoirs,* Vol. 2, Pt. 3. Lancaster, 1908.

——. *Songs of the Tewa.* Exposition of Indian Tribal Arts. New York, 1933.

——. In *Folk Tales of Salishan and Sahaptin Tribes,* ed. by Franz Boas. Lancaster, Pa., 1917.

STEVENSON, MATHILDE COX. *The Religious Life of the Zuñi Child.* 5th Annual Report of the Bureau of American Ethnology. Washington, 1887.

——. *The Sia.* 11th *ibid.,* 1894.

STEWARD, JULIAN H. *Two Paiute Autobiographies. University of California Publications in American Archaeology and Ethnology,* Vol. 33, Pt. 5. Berkeley, 1934.

SWANTON, JOHN R. *Tlingit Myths and Texts.* 39th Annual Report of the Bureau of American Ethnology. Washington, 1909.

SIMMONS, LEO W., ed. *Sun Chief, The Autobiography of a Hopi Indian.* Institute of Human Relations. New Haven: Yale University Press, 1942.

TEIT, JAMES. In *Folktales of Salishan and Sahaptin Tribes,* ed. by Franz Boas. Lancaster, Pa.: 1917.

THOMPSON, J. ERIC. *The Mayas of Southern and Central British Honduras. Field Museum of Natural History, Anthropological Series,* Vol. 17. Chicago, 1927.

UNDERHILL, RUTH. *The Autobiography of a Papago Woman.* The American Anthropological Association, *Memoirs,* Vol. 46. Menasha, 1936.

——. *Singing for Power, the Song Magic of the Papago Indians of Southern Arizona.* Berkeley, 1938.

WISSLER, CLARK. *Mythology of the Blackfoot Indians. Anthropological Papers of the American Museum of Natural History,* Vol. 2. New York, 1908.

——. *Ceremonial Bundles of the Blackfoot Indians. Ibid.,* Vol. 7, 1912.

THE INDIAN AS AUTHOR

Selected titles of books written or dedicated by aborigines of America [1]

From the Plains

1. *The Autobiography of Black Hawk,* 1838, ed. by J. B. Patterson, 1882. (Sac).

[1] For a complete list see Clyde Kluckhohn, "The Personal Document in Anthropological Science," in Gottschalk, *The Use of Personal Documents* (New York: Social Science Research Council, 1945), pp. 164–173.

2. CHARLES A. EASTMAN (Ohiyesa)
   From the Deep Woods to Civilization: chapters in the autobiography of an Indian. Boston: Little, Brown, 1916.
   The Soul of the Indian. Boston and New York: Houghton Mifflin, 1911.
3. *American, the life story of a great Indian,* by Frank B. Linderman. New York: The John Day Company, 1930.
4. *Black Elk Speaks, The Life Story of an Oglala Sioux,* as told to John G. Neihardt. New York, 1932.
5. *Chief Longlance Buffalo Child,* autobiography. New York: Cosmopolitan Book Corp., 1928.
6. *The Autobiography of a Fox Woman,* ed. by Truman Michelson. *Annual Report of the Bureau of American Ethnology.* No. 40, 1918-19.
7. CHIEF STANDING BEAR. *The Land of the Spotted Eagle.* Boston and New York: Houghton Mifflin, 1933.
8. *Crashing Thunder, the Autobiography of an American Indian,* ed. by Paul Radin. New York: D. Appleton, 1926.

From the Northwest

CHARLES JAMES NOWELL (Kwakiutl). *Smoke from Their Fires,* ed. by Chellan S. Ford. New Haven: Yale University Press, 1940.

From the Southwest

1. DON C. TALAYESVA. *Sun Chief, Autobiography of a Hopi,* ed. by Leo W. Simmons. New Haven: Yale University Press, 1942.

2. *Autobiography of a Papago Woman,* ed. by Ruth Underhill. The American Anthropological Association, *Memoirs,* Vol. 46, 1936.

3. *Two Paiute Autobiographies,* as told to Julian H. Steward. *University of California Publications in American Archaeology and Ethnology,* Vol. 33, No. 5, 1934.

4. *Son of Old Man Flat,* a Navajo autobiography recorded by Walter Dyk. New York: Harcourt, Brace & Co., 1938.

INDEX

Acculturation, 53 seq.; 252 seq. (Hopi); 319 seq. (Zapotec); see also Christianity

Acoma, 56 (pantheon), 64

Adjustment, 252 seq. (Hopi)

Allouez, Father, 54

Amassalik Eskimo, 31; see also Eskimo

Ancestors, 169 (Delaware); see also Spirits of the dead; Katcinas; Koshairi

Apache, 13

Assiniboine, 93 seq.

Atkinson, General, 141, 142

Balam, Books of Chilam, 329 seq.

Baptism, ritual of, 54 seq.

Benedict, Ruth, 6 (Zuñi mythology), 224, 242

Big House Ceremony, Delaware, 166 seq.; 169 (symbolism)

Black Elk, 41, 132

Blackfoot Indians, 42

Black Hawk, 136 seq.

Boas, Franz, 7, 16

Bogoras, V., 21

Brinton, Daniel G., 5, 311

Bundle, sacred, 114, 154, 155

Bunzel, Ruth, 9 (translations from the Zuñi); 232 (Zuñi ritual poetry)

Catharsis (through song), 30

Cherokee Indians, 176 seq.

Children, 39 seq. (education in quietude and reticence); 108, 244 (education)

Chippewa Indians, 22, 27; 37 seq. (psychotherapy); 46 (songs received during a vision); 49 (death song)

Christianity, 53 seq. (influence on aboriginal culture); 85 seq.; 145 (Ghost Dance); 163; 244 seq. (Hopi); 319 seq. (Zapotec); 329 seq. (Books of Chilam Balam); 331 seq. (Maya); 333; 334 seq.

Climate and language, 9

Clouds (and spirits of the dead), 227

Clowning, ceremonial, 35

Contest song, 30 seq.

Contrast and parallel phrasing, 14

Corn, 106 seq. (Pawnee worship of Mother-Corn); 233 (Zuñi); see also Maize

Corn Dance in Santo Domingo, 32 seq.

Council Song (Teton Sioux), 124

Coyote, 117 seq. (—and origin of death: Caddo); 118 seq.; 261 (—and origin of death); 270

Creation Myth, 96 seq. (Osage); 240 seq. (Zuñi); 263 (Luiseño); 267 seq. (Maricopa); 278 seq. (Wishosk); 290 seq. (—related during mourning ceremony: Tlingit); 326 (Uitoto)

Crow Indians, 10; 15 (ora-

JUN 1	1995 DATE DUE		

398.208

The Winged serpent